INSTRUMENTATION

An Introduction
for Students
in the Speech
and Hearing Sciences

Second Edition

INSTRUMENTATION

An Introduction
for Students
in the Speech
and Hearing Sciences

Second Edition

T. Newell Decker

University of Nebraska—Lincoln

LAWRENCE ERLBAUM ASSOCIATES, PUBLISHERS
1996   Mahwah, New Jersey

Lawrence Erlbaum Associates, Inc., Publishers
10 Industrial Avenue
Mahwah, New Jersey 07430

Cover design by Gail Silverman

Library of Congress Cataloging-in-Publication Data

Decker, T. Newell.
    Instrumentation : an introduction for students in the speech and
hearing sciences / T. Newell Decker. — 2nd ed.
       p.   cm.
    Includes bibliographical references and index.
    ISBN 0-8058-2186-4 (pbk. : alk. paper)
    1. Speech therapy—Instruments.   2. Audiology—Instruments.
I. Title.
RC429.D37   1996
616.05′506—dc20   95-47826
                                                                CIP

Books published by Lawrence Erlbaum Associates are printed
on acid-free paper, and their bindings are chosen for strength
and durability.

Printed in the United States of America
10 9 8 7 6 5 4 3 2 1

for S. L. Decker

Contents

Illustrations

Preface to the Second Edition

It has been 6 years since the publication of the first edition of *Instrumentation*. One might reasonably ask, "What has changed in the area of basic instrumentation in the last 5 or 6 years?" The answer, I think, would be "Not very much and yet quite a bit!"

The basic items of instrumentation that are used in the hearing and speech sciences are still pretty much the same. The major difference is the ever-increasing use of microprocessors and software. Many of the traditional "stand-alone" instruments have been replaced by the desktop computer. Through software the computer is able to mimic many different pieces of "virtual" equipment. A single desktop computer today might serve as an augmentative communication device, an audiometer, a typanometer, a speech analysis instrument, and an oscilloscope. Furthermore, it might be called upon to do all of these things in a single day!

Because of the increased importance of digital manipulation of our data collection and record keeping, I have rearranged some of the chapters in this edition. For example, Chapters 8 and 10 have been moved forward in the book to provide the reader with better background for later chapters. Beyond this and a few other minor additions and deletions, readers of this second edition will not find it far different from the first one.

My thanks again to all of my colleagues who have provided helpful suggestions and words of encouragement. Special thank yous go to all of the students who have indicated to me that "the book helped" in their study and understanding of instrumentation. That, after all, was the reason for this effort.

— *T. Newell Decker*

Preface to the First Edition

This text is intended to be an introductory and practical guide to instrumentation for the undergraduate and beginning graduate student in speech pathology and audiology. Given the rapid development of technology in these fields, it must be realized that this book is not intended to be the "last word" on instrumentation, nor can it take the place of a patient and knowledgeable instructor. Rather, you should use it as a key to unlock the door to a vault of far more difficult information associated with the understanding and use of instrumentation.

I have kept difficult formulas, figures, and tables to a minimum so that you will not be distracted from the introductory nature of the discussions. I have included a list of important terms and references for more advanced reading in each chapter. In chapters where it appeared appropriate, I have included lab exercises so that you may quickly apply what you read. For the most part, these exercises are intended to be accomplished without the aid of an instructor.

To make the concepts involved in the use of instrumentation understandable, it is important to have some basic knowledge of electricity and electrical terms, hence the inclusion of Chapter 1. This is the only chapter in which there are more than one or two formulas. However, the formulas are well explained and are accompanied by examples. I do not think that you will be overwhelmed by them. Chapter 2 is a discussion of ways instruments can be interconnected into a working system, and it contains useful information on the use of patch cords and soldering. This chapter will, I hope, give you the necessary help in learning to think of individual pieces of equipment as parts of a larger system. Chapters 3 through 7 are devoted to discussions of major workhorse pieces of instrumentation that are common in the speech and hearing clinic or laboratory. These pieces of equipment are the basic building blocks that you will use over and over as your knowledge of instrumentation increases. Chapter 9 is aimed directly at the speech pathology student. In recent years there has been a vast increase in the use of instrumentation in the speech clinic. Instruments that were once available only to the sophisticated speech scientist are now available to the clinician in the form of dedicated microprocessor-based systems. Although Chapter 8 contains a good deal of specific information about the sound spectrograph, it and Chapter 10 contain information that is more generic to the broad scope of work that we do as speech and hearing professionals. Spectrum analysis and digital signal processing are intimately related, and they provide us with powerful tools for new understanding of the communication process.

Many people have contributed to this book on one level or another. Dr. Bruce Weber of Duke University provided me free access to his laboratory and abundant mentoring skills while he was at the University of Washington and I was a doctoral student. A good deal of credit goes to my students who over the years have asked the challenging questions that have led me to acquire new knowledge. I especially want to thank Dr. John Bernthal who, as chair of my department, has in the past few years provided valuable financial and philosophical support for my laboratory activities. Although I am sure that he has on occasion viewed my lab as the department "money pit," he has not wavered in his understanding of the need for up-to-date equipment. In that same light, I also wish to acknowledge the continuing support of the Research Council of the University of Nebraska at Lincoln. Drs. E. Charles Healey and David R. Beukelman gave me invaluable assistance and advice for Chapters 8 and 9. Richard Young provided his expertise in preparing some of the photographic material for the book. I also thank the various authors, corporations, and publishers for their permission in allowing me to reproduce many of the figures in the text.

Finally and especially, I would like to thank my wife, Claudia, for her patience and understanding during all those hours that I spent upstairs on the word processor and away from my family.

— T. Newell Decker

Introduction

Why read a book about electricity and basic instrumentation? Why take a class on the topic? For that matter, why go to the trouble of writing a book on the subject? Perhaps I can supply some reasons worth considering.

Early in my education as an audiologist and a student of auditory physiology, I discovered that I seemed to have a special interest in the area of instrumentation. This fascination with gadgets caused me to investigate certain areas of speech pathology and audiology from which, under other circumstances, I might otherwise have stayed away. Over the years, however, I have seen many students who did not possess this same fascination and who instead showed a great deal of anxiety when faced with various forms of instrumentation. Many of these students did not develop skills in the use of instrumentation and consequently missed out on some of the more fascinating areas of their chosen disciplines. It has always seemed to me that if some of these less adventurous students could have been given a basic (and fairly painless) understanding of electronics and instrumentation, those fears would have disappeared, or would have at least been dissipated, and a new world of adventure would have opened for them.

Another concern I have had over the years is with the student or practicing clinician who does not take advantage, or does not know how to take advantage, of some of the electrical advances and their attendant time savings. I often talk with students and clinicians who use tape recorders only for playback of prerecorded material because they don't know the first thing about making recordings. I see the speech pathologist or audiologist who shies away from the use of spectrographs, auditory trainers, oscilloscopes, and filters because he or she has no idea how these devices work or how they might be adapted to special needs. I am frequently asked by students to "show me what's wrong" with an instrumentation setup because they have not learned to troubleshoot on their own.

While it is true that some will always have more use than others for electronics, no one in speech pathology and audiology can say that electronics has no place in what they do. Electronics has become a fact of life in modern society and its application to an enormous variety of human endeavors has helped to expand our knowledge exponentially. In the fields of speech pathology and audiology, electronic applications have not only broadened the reach of the basic and applied scientist but have created a whole new clinical armamentarium for the practitioner. So it is important to understand how these electronic tools work and, more important, how they can be made to work for us.

After reading this text, I hope you will be more confident with instrumentation and more willing to experiment with it. I also hope that you will be able to appreciate the possible ways that electronic instrumentation can be used in your work.

I wrote this book with the undergraduate in speech and hearing sciences uppermost in my mind. My experience has been that the typical undergraduate in the discipline has a limited science background; therefore I assumed the reader has very little prior knowledge of electronics. Instead of detailed information about individual pieces of instrumentation, I have used a more basic and broad descriptive approach. Throughout the book, I have tried to give examples of how certain pieces of equipment can be used in the clinic or laboratory. One or more step-by-step exercises are included at the end of certain chapters to help students obtain hands-on experience. Equipment flowcharts help reinforce the exercise. For the most part these exercises can be done without the help of your instructor. I hope that you will undertake these simple exercises and, in so doing, find that instruments do not "bite" and, in fact, can be fun to use.

Terms that are defined in the glossary are boldfaced in the text. These terms are listed at the end of the chapter in which they appear so you can review them as you conclude each chapter. At the end of each chapter there is also a partial list of more advanced reference material for the instrumentation discussed. These references can be read in depth or simply sampled for additional information. In addition, these references have been compiled at the end of the book.

It is my intent that students who complete this book will have a basic understanding of the major pieces of instrumentation in the hearing and speech clinic/laboratory. Furthermore, it is my hope that students who read this book and wish to know more about instrumentation will find that this text has given them the background to be able to understand and profit from reading more advanced texts.

CHAPTER 1

Introduction to Basic Electricity

Almost without exception when a person decides to use an instrument, it must first be connected to an electrical outlet. Because electricity is almost always available for our use, we tend to take it for granted, never questioning what it is or from where it comes. There are, however, some fundamental electrical concepts that are important to the overall understanding of clinical and laboratory equipment as it is discussed in later chapters of this book. But even more important, these concepts should be understood in order to operate instruments safely. This chapter contains a simplified discussion of where electricity comes from, what its basic parameters are, and how it can be used safely. Some simple equations and formulas illustrate the basic concepts, and you are encouraged to study them.

ELECTRICAL FIELDS AND CHARGES

Atoms are no longer thought of as the smallest particle of an element. We now know that atoms are made up of much smaller particles, some of which are: **electrons, protons,** and **neutrons.** Electrons and protons are the stuff of which electrical energy is made. Electrons have an electrical charge with a negative value, whereas protons have an electrical charge with a positive value. Both protons and electrons are of fundamental importance to the presence of electricity. Because neutrons have a neutral or zero charge, we will not be concerned with them in this chapter.

Figure 1.1 demonstrates a basic characteristic of electrical charges. Charges that are of the same value, or sign, repel; charges that are of different values or signs attract. Most of us have demonstrated this property to ourselves with magnets. If we hold the south poles of two magnets together and then release them, the magnets jump apart. If, on the other hand, we hold the south pole of one magnet and the north pole of the other magnet close together and then release them, they jump together. There is a **field of force** (attraction) between the magnets just as there is with the electrical charges. This force field pushes like charges away and attracts dissimilar charges. By convention, this field of force is usually visualized from the perspective of the positive electrical charge. Figure 1.2 shows the field of force as arrows pushing away from the positive charge and pushing toward the negative charge. In other words, if the charge is positive, the direction of the force field is away from it; if the charge is negative, the direction of the force field is toward it.

Figure 1.3 shows a force field between two plates, one with a positive charge and one with a negative charge. Arrows show the direction of the electrical field of force, and a single, movable charge is midway between the two plates. The charge is being pushed down away from the top plate and pulled down toward the bottom plate. It is important to remember that the force of the field is constant anywhere between the two plates. That is, the farther away from the positive plate the charge moves, the less force is exerted from the top, but an increased force of equal strength pulls from the bottom. For example, if the charge is subjected to a force of two newtons at point A, it is also subjected to a force of two newtons at point B and point C. Midway between the two

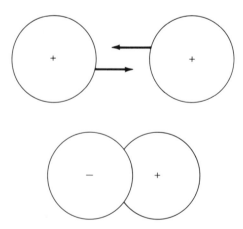

Figure 1.1 Polarity of electrical charges showing that different charges attract and similar charges repel.

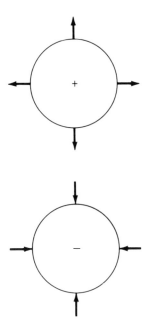

Figure 1.2   Electrical fields of force.

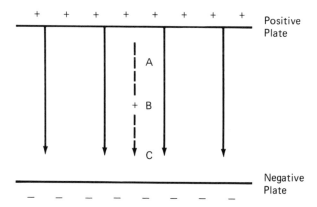

Figure 1.3   The relationship between a movable electrical charge and the electrical field. (Source: Adapted from *Resistive and Reactive Circuits,* Albert P. Malvino. New York: McGraw Hill, 1974, p. 18.)

plates, the downward push equals the downward pull. When the positive charge is closer to the upper plate, the downward push is stronger than the pull, but the sum of the two equals the same value as when the charge was at the midpoint. The same is true if the charge is closer to the bottom plate because now the downward pull is greater than the downward push.

Another way to set up a constant electrical field is with a battery. When a wire is connected across the poles of the battery, it produces a constant electrical field inside the wire. Any movable charge inside the wire feels the force of the poles of the battery. The force then pushes the charges through the wire—that is, causes electricity to flow.

At this point it is reasonable to ask, "Where do these electrons or charges that travel through the wire come from?" Before answering this question directly, let's briefly discuss the makeup of an atom. Basically, the atom is made up of a core, or nucleus, of protons (which are positively charged), neutrons (which have no charge), and a series of orbiting electrons (which are negatively charged). An atom of copper, for example, has a nucleus of 29 protons and 29 orbiting electrons. Therefore, the net charge of the copper atom is neutral. There is a balance between the charge in the nucleus and that of the orbiting shell of electrons. The outermost orbiting electron is so far away from the nucleus that it is not strongly held in its position, and it is easy to dislodge the outer orbiting electron from the copper atom. Dislodging this outer orbit electron leaves a positively charged atom because there are now more positively charged protons than negatively charged electrons. Certain types of metals make better conductors of electricity than others because they have electrons in their outer orbits that are easily dislodged. These metals (gold, silver, copper, platinum) have **free electrons** that can be made to move from one nucleus to another with little effort.

Figure 1.4 shows a piece of wire containing five nuclei, or cores, and five orbiting outer electrons. If we place positive charges on one end of the wire and negative charges on the other end, a constant electrical field is set up. The net result is that the field will try to force the cores to the right and pull the free electrons to the left. *Remember:* Like charges repel and opposite charges attract.

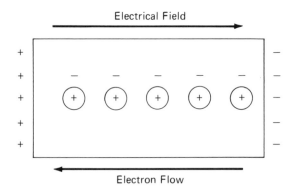

Figure 1.4 The effect of the electrical field on the atomic nuclei and electron shells of the conductor. (Source: Adapted from *Resistive and Reactive Circuits,* Albert P. Malvino. New York: McGraw Hill, 1974, p. 16.)

We said that the field will try to force the nuclei to the right, but they will be held fast in position because they are tightly packed against the other nuclei of other atoms. The free electrons, however, will move easily to the left (toward the positive charge), leaving positive cores at the right end of the wire. Other free electrons can then enter the right end of the wire and go into orbit around the positive cores. At the same time, free electrons leave the left end of the wire, and so on and on, producing a continuous flow of free electrons through the wire. From this discussion it should be clear that the flow of current (free electrons) is in opposition to the direction of the field of force, or electrical field. The flow of electrical current is always from negative to positive, and the direction of the electrical field is always positive to negative.

AC AND DC CURRENT

The electrical energy that flows in a conductor can be generated in either of two ways: One form is called **alternating current (AC)** and the other **direct current (DC)**. The voltage in an alternating current circuit is constantly changing from zero to some maximum and then back again in one direction, and then it does the same in the opposite direction. As schematized in Figure 1.5a, the result is a sinusoidal function relating amplitude to time. In the United States the periodicity of this signal is 60 **hertz (Hz)**, meaning that the polarity of the signal reverses 60 times each second. When equipment is not properly grounded, we sometimes hear this signal as a low pitched hum.

In DC circuits the amount and direction of the voltage are always constant, with either a positive or negative value. Direct current is most often produced

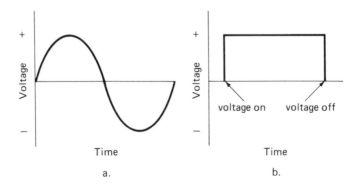

Figure 1.5 A schematic representation of (a) alternating current and (b) direct current.

by batteries. Because batteries are a convenient and portable method of storing electricity, direct current is usually the power on which portable equipment runs. Figure 1.5b shows DC current coming on with a positive polarity, staying constant, and then being turned off and returning to zero volts.

CURRENT, VOLTAGE, RESISTANCE

Current, voltage, and resistance are three fundamental factors present in every electrical circuit. Therefore, it is important that you have a basic understanding of each.

Current

The word *current* refers to running or flowing, and in electrical terms it means a flowing of free electrons. **Current (Q)** is defined as the number of free electrons that pass through a given point divided by the time that it takes them to pass. Measuring the passage of a single electron would be a formidable task, so a much larger quantity is needed. This standard quantity is the **coulomb (C)** which is the metric measure for electric charge. One coulomb equals the electric charge that exists or the amount of electricity present on 6.24×10^{18} protons or electrons. The formula for finding the charge in coulombs is

$$Q = \frac{n}{6.24} \times 10^{18} \qquad \text{Eq. 1.1}$$

where

$\quad$ Q = the charge in coulombs
$\quad$ n = the number of protons or electrons.

The charge in coulombs becomes simply a ratio between a given number of electrons and a standard reference. Current, as we have said, refers to a rate of flow. Now that we have established the size of the charge, we want to know the value of this charge over time (current). For this we call on the unit known as the **ampere (amp)**. The ampere, or amp, is the metric unit measure for current, or charge over time, and 1 amp equals 1 C per second. Therefore, if the flow of electrons is 1 C per second, the current has a value of 1 amp. For example, if 9×10^{18} electrons pass through a section of wire in 5 sec, how much current measured in coulombs is there, and what is the current?

If

$$Q = \frac{n}{6.24} \times 10^{18}$$

$$Q = 9 \times \frac{10^{18}}{6.24} \times 10^{18}$$

then

$$Q = 1.44$$

If

$$amp = \frac{Q}{s}$$

where

$$s = time\ in\ seconds$$

and

$$Q = 1.44$$

then

$$amp = \frac{1.44}{5}$$

or

$$amp = 0.288\ amps,\ or\ 2.88\ milliamps.$$

To review, current is defined as the number of total protons or electrons divided by the standard number of protons or electrons in 1 C. Current (Q) is defined as the rate of electron flow in coulombs per second and is expressed in amperes.

Voltage

Much as the flow of water through a hose is dependent on the pressure or force with which the water is made to flow, electrical current in a conductor depends on the force pushing the free electrons. **Force** is defined as mass times acceleration. The greater the force, the larger the current. Voltage, which is a measure of force, is analogous to pressure. For a clearer understanding of voltage, take a closer look at several other related concepts. The first of these is **work (J)**. The usual unit of measure for work is the **joule (J)**. Work is done when a force (F) moves through a distance (D).

$$work\ (J) = Force\ (F) \times Distance\ (D)$$

$$J = FD \hspace{4cm} Eq.\ 1.2$$

One J equals 1 newton-meter. In other words, 1 J is the amount of work done when a force of 1 newton moves a distance of 1 m. A **newton (N)** is a measure of force equal to 0.225 lbs.

The second concept is that of **potential energy**. A body has potential energy if it can do (has the potential to do) work on another body. Furthermore, the amount of energy a body has equals the work it can do. If a body has 12 J of energy, it can do 12 J of work. Figure 1.6 illustrates these concepts. The figure shows a body that "weighs" 100 newtons. If it is released from its position in

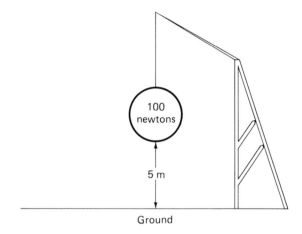

Figure 1.6 The potential energy of a movable mass illustrating the concept of work equaling force multiplied by distance.

the figure, it will push down with a force of 100 newtons and move through a distance of 5 m. How much work will be accomplished?

$$J = FD$$

$$= 100 \times 5$$

$$= 500 \; J$$

The amount of work that this body can do is equal to 500 J. Therefore, this elevated body has a potential energy of 500 J with respect to its position relative to the ground. To put this statement into electrical terms, examine Figure 1.7, which shows a body (positive charge of 2 C) that is being pushed down on by the electrical field with a force at point B equal to 3 newtons. If the charge is released, it will exert a downward force of 3 newtons through a distance of 1 m. Therefore, the charge has a potential energy of

$$J = FD$$

$$= 3 \times$$

$$= 3 \; J \; \text{(relative to the bottom plate, or ground).}$$

If we now move the charge to point A, it will exert a force of 3 newtons through a distance of 5 m, giving it a potential energy of 15 J. The difference in potential energy at points A and B (12 J) equals the work the charge can do as it moves from one point to another.

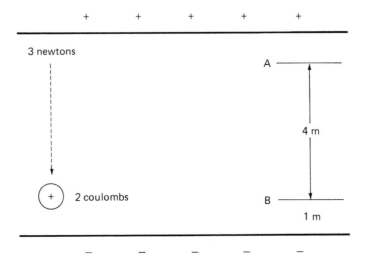

Figure 1.7 The potential energy of a charge between two electrical poles. (Source: Adapted from *Resistive and Reactive Circuits,* Albert P. Malvino. New York: McGraw Hill, 1974, p. 31.)

We can now better define voltage. The voltage (v) between two points is the difference in potential energy divided by the charge.

$$\frac{\text{voltage (v)} = \text{(J)}}{\text{charge (Q)}}$$ Eq. 1.3

Figure 1.7 shows that the voltage between points A and B can be expressed as

$$v = \frac{J}{Q}$$

$$= \frac{12J}{2Q}$$

$$= 6J/C \text{ (6 joules per charge in coulombs)}$$

The metric unit of voltage is the volt (v).

1 v = 1 J per coulomb (C)

A **volt (v)** is the amount of potential energy that exists between two points when each coulomb of charge can do 1 joule of work as it moves between the two points. We have calculated the voltage between points A and B as 6 J/C; we can now convert this expression to one with more common terms.

$$6J/C = 6 \times 1 \, J/C = 6 \times 1 \, v = 6 \, v$$

When voltage applied to a circuit is multiplied by the current in amperes, the result is units of power called watts. The **watt (w)** is a unit of power and indicates the rate at which the load is consuming the power.

$$\text{power (w)} = \text{volts (v)} \times \text{amperes (amp)} \qquad \text{Eq. 1.4}$$

Resistance

Resistance is a property of the material that composes the circuit and is a measure of the number of free electrons in the circuit. In general, the larger the amount of free electrons, the lower the resistance. Material used in electrical circuits can be classified as either **conductors, semiconductors,** or **insulators.** A conductor has a large amount of free electrons, whereas a semiconductor is composed of material with certain impurities that represent themselves as "holes" in the atomic structure. These holes can remain vacant or be filled by electrons, depending on the circuit design. Thus, semiconductors can be used to regulate the flow of current. Finally, insulators are composed of material in which the atoms are tightly bound to one another and not free to move.

Any device that is connected across an energy source and provides resistance to the flow of current is called a load. If electrical charges move easily through the load, it is said to have low resistance; if not, the load has high resistance. The **resistance** of a load is defined as the voltage across the load divided by the current through the load.

$$\text{resistance (r)} = \text{voltage (v)}/\text{amperes (amp)} \qquad \text{Eq. 1.5}$$

For example, if the voltage across a load equals 12 v and the current is 2 amp, the resistance is equal to:

$$r = v/amp$$

$$= 12/2$$

$$= 6 \text{ v per amp.}$$

The usual expression of resistance is the ohm (Ω).

$$1 \text{ ohm } (\Omega) = 1 \text{ volt (v)}/\text{ampere (amp)}$$

therefore:

$$6 \text{ v/amp} = 6 \times 1 \text{ v/amp} = 6 \times 1 \, \Omega = 6 \, \Omega.$$

Resistance in a device is usually manifested as a rise in temperature. The resistance makes it possible for the electrical energy to be converted to other forms of energy (light, heat, mechanical motion, etc.). The load resistance determines how much current will flow in the circuit. Increase the resistance, and the current flowing in the circuit will automatically be decreased. Resistors are made to be capable of introducing specific levels of resistance into an electrical circuit. These values are indicated on the resistor by a series of color-coded bands. The coding scheme is illustrated in Figure 1.8.

INDUCTANCE AND CAPACITANCE

Inductance

Recall that in the opening lines of this chapter we discussed electrical fields of force and discussed them as magnetic fields, for indeed there is a magnetic field around any conductor in which electricity is flowing. **Inductance** is a property of these magnetic lines of force. The lines of force that surround the circuit are usually referred to as **electrical flux** and are measured in a metric unit called the **weber (Wb)**. The amount of inductance in a circuit depends on the amount of flux and the size of the current.

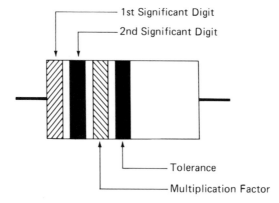

Color	Significant Figure	Multiplication Factor	Percentage of Tolerance
Black	0		
Brown	1	1	
Red	2	10	
Orange	3	100	
Yellow	4	1,000	
Green	5	10,000	
Blue	6	100,000	
Violet	7	1,000,000	
Gray	8	10,000,000	
White	9	1,000,000,000	
Gold	—	0.1	± 5
Silver	—	0.01	± 10
No Color	—		± 20

Figure 1.8   Resistor color codes.

The metric unit of inductance, the **henry (H),** is therefore, given as:

$$1 \text{ henry (H)} = 1 \text{ weber (Wb)/amperes (amp)} \qquad \text{Eq. 1.6}$$

Inductors are commonly constructed by coiling wire around a core of soft iron and are used to change voltage or to isolate one portion of an electrical circuit from another. Opposition to the flow of current in an inductor is called **inductive reactance.** Either an increase in the inductance or increase in the frequency of the signal will serve to increase the reactance and thus decrease current flow. The usual example of inductive reactance and its effects is given by reference to a large mass versus a small mass. It is much easier to move a small mass (paper clip) than it is to move a large mass (automobile). So, the effort needed to sustain movement (current flow) goes up either as the mass (inductance) is increased or as the rate of movement (frequency) is increased. Stated very simply, inductive reactance works against or opposes the flow of high frequency current.

Capacitance

Capacitance is the measure of the amount of charge that can be stored in a capacitor and is expressed in **farads.** A farad is expressed as follows:

$$1 \text{ farad (F)} = 1 \text{ coulomb (C)/volts (v).} \qquad \text{Eq. 1.7}$$

A capacitor is constructed from two metal plates that are separated by a nonconducting material. When electricity is applied to a circuit containing a capacitor, current flows through the circuit but not across the capacitor. As a result, electrons build up on one of the plates of the capacitor until the net charge on the plate equals that of the electrical source and current flow stops. If the polarity of the current is then reversed, the current begins to flow again and electrons begin to build up on the opposite plate of the capacitor. It follows then that the higher the frequency of the current, the greater will be the flow since neither plate of the capacitor will have time to fill. The opposition to the flow of current through a capacitor is called **capacitive reactance.** Perhaps the best analogy for capacitors and for capacitive reactance is a mechanical spring. When first compressed a spring provides little opposition but upon further compression the opposition becomes greater. The spring will provide little opposition to rapid but minimal amounts of compression whereas slower and more complete compression will result in greater opposition to force. Because of this property, capacitors can be used in a circuit to block the flow of low-frequency current, which can be useful in certain applications when one wishes low frequency filtering.

WHERE DOES ELECTRICAL ENERGY COME FROM?

Recall that for electricity to flow there must be an imbalance between the net positive charge and the net negative charge. Electricity is generated by causing all the free electrons in a conductor to move in the same direction. To accomplish this there must be at some beginning point a generator with two outputs. One of these outputs must maintain an oversupply of free electrons (negative pole), and the other must maintain an undersupply of free electrons (positive pole). If this fundamental condition is maintained, whenever a device (load) is connected across these two outputs (no matter how distant from the source), electricity will flow through the device.

WHAT IS AN ELECTRICAL CIRCUIT?

As previously discussed, a closed path of electron movement is needed to have electric energy in a useful form. This closed path is called an **electrical circuit** and consists of four basic elements: source, conductor, load, and switch.

1. **Source.** The original source is some electrical generator, but for practical purposes the source may be thought of as the wall outlet.
2. **Conductor.** Conductors are wires that carry the electrical current to the load that will use it. Conductors offer little resistance to the flow of current because the metals they are made of are rich in a supply of free electrons.
3. **Load.** The load is any device that uses the electrical current. The load, unlike the conductor, offers resistance to the flow of the current.
4. **Switch.** This unit in the system provides a method for controlling the energy. A switch controls current flow by placing a very high resistance (air gap) in the way of the current flow when the switch is opened. When the switch is closed, the resistance is removed.

OPEN CIRCUITS AND SHORT CIRCUITS

An open circuit is a fault, intentional or otherwise, that disrupts the flow of current in the conductor. The break (discontinuity) that occurs may take place in either of the two wires of the conductor or in the load device.

A short circuit is a fault that occurs when a low-resistance path exists between one of the wires of the conductor and some point where the current can flow into the earth. This path of least resistance often takes place between the conductor and the case, or housing, of the load device. There is the possibility of actually having one's body become part of the circuit — perhaps with disastrous results.

GROUNDING

Grounding can prevent open circuits and short circuits. To **ground** means to connect or to provide a path along which the electricity can flow into the earth. The earth is such a huge volume of matter that a surplus or shortage of electrons never exists. The earth, or ground, is therefore always electrically neutral. Whenever the normal low-resistance path of the current is disrupted by a short circuit, the usual result is that the electricity is made to flow in a path with lower resistance than that of the path through the load. Because electricity naturally seeks the path of least resistance, stray current from a short will be shunted to ground (if the device is grounded) rather than run through a higher resistance pathway such as the human body.

KEY TERMS

alternating current (AC)	henry (H)
ampere (amp)	hertz (Hz)
capacitance	inductance
capacitive reactance	inductive reactance
conductor	insulator
coulomb (C)	joule (J)
current (Q)	load
direct current (DC)	newton (N)
electrical circuit	neutron
electrical flux	ohm (Ω)
electron	potential energy
farad (F)	proton
field of force	resistance (r)
free electron	semiconductor
ground	source
	switch
	volts (voltage) (v)
	watts (wattage) (w)
	weber (Wb)
	work (J)

SUGGESTED READINGS

Curtis, Jack F., and Martin C. Schultz. *Basic Laboratory Instrumentation for Speech and Hearing*. Boston: Little, Brown, 1986.

Dawson, William L. *Instrumentation in the Speech Clinic*. Danville, IL: Interstate Printers & Publishers, 1973.

Departments of the Army and Air Force. *Electrical Fundamentals.* Department of the Army Technical Manual (TM11–681) and Department of the Air Force Technical Order (TO 16-1-218). Departments of the Army and Air Force, 1976.

Malmstadt, Howard V., Christie G. Enke, and Stanley R. Crouch. *Electronics and Instrumentation for Scientists*, Menlo Park, CA : Benjamin/Cummings Pub. Co., 1981.

Malvino, Albert P. *Resistive and Reactive Circuits.* New York: McGraw-Hill, 1974.

McPherson, David L., and John W. Thatcher. *Instrumentation in the Hearing Sciences.* New York: Grune & Stratton, 1977.

Young, Stephen. *Electronics in the Life Sciences.* New York: Halsted Press, 1973.

CHAPTER 2

Combining Equipment into Arrays

In the laboratory or in the clinic, it is rare to see a piece of instrumentation standing alone to accomplish a specific task. More often than not two, three, or more individual instruments must be interconnected to accomplish the task at hand. As an example, to record a sample of speech you may need to connect a microphone to a tape recorder. Then, to play back that speech sample, you may need an amplifier and a loudspeaker connected to the tape recorder.

INTERCONNECTION OF EQUIPMENT

When faced with the task of connecting several pieces of equipment, the beginning user will often despair because of not knowing what to connect to what. The most basic instruction is that the output of one piece of instrumentation is to be connected to the input of the next. In most instances, the inputs and outputs of instruments are clearly marked so that all you need do is to find the correct type of connecting cords (this is discussed more fully later in this chapter). On some pieces of equipment there are two inputs: one marked "mic" and the other marked "line." The reasons for these two inputs will become obvious later in this chapter when we talk about the concepts of impedance and impedance matching. For now it is enough to understand that a microphone, because of its very small output signal, must be connected to a special type of input. Usually this mic input will provide some amplification to the signal before it is passed on to the rest of the instrumentation. Connections made from another piece of instrumentation on which the output signal is already amplified should be made at the line input, which is specially designed to handle such signals. An example of such a situation is connecting the output signal of a tape recorder to the input of another tape recorder. Because the tape recorder output amplifies the signal to some degree (to a line level of about 1 v), there is no need for additional amplification at the input of the second tape recorder.

Logic usually dictates the sequence of connection. As an example, suppose that you wish to record a sample of your own voice and that you wish the recorded segment to contain only the lower frequencies of the speech signal. You will need a microphone to pick up the signal, connected to an amplifier to boost the amplitude of the signal. Next, you must route the amplified signal to some sort of filter, to filter out the higher frequencies. Finally, you must send the amplified, filtered signal to the input of the tape recorder. This is a simple example; nonetheless, it illustrates the type of logical thought that is necessary when you interconnect equipment. It is often helpful to draw the sequencing of the equipment on a piece of paper before actually confronting the hardware. In fact, a casual look through journal articles reveals that even the seasoned investigator often produces such drawings so that the reader will have an easier time understanding the instrumentation.

IMPEDANCE AND IMPEDANCE MATCHING

Besides connecting the output of one piece of equipment to the input of another, you must obtain the most efficient connection possible at the point of energy transfer between the two. Energy transfer between equipment is best when the output characteristics of one instrument match the input characteristics of the second instrument. This care for input-output characteristics is called **impedance matching**. Equation 2.1 can be used to calculate the amount of energy that will be transferred from one system to another.

$$X = Z_b Z_a / (Z_b + Z_a)$$
Eq. 2.1

In this equation X refers to the energy transferred, Z_a refers to the characteristic impedance of the first system, and Z_b refers to that for the second. We will refer to this equation later in this chapter.

The term **impedance** refers to the opposition of an electrical circuit to the flow of alternating current (AC) through that circuit. Because every piece of electronic equipment has individual characteristics (in the same manner as musical instruments), it will have a characteristic impedance. The characteristic impedance will be the sum of the equipment's individual inductances and capacitances (see Chapter 1). If these characteristics do not match between pieces of equipment, an impedance mismatch will exist that will result in a loss of power or distortion of the signals as they pass through the systems. Because it is important to have the most faithful transmission possible through our instruments, we must take some care to match the impedances. However, complete matching of impedances is important only when interconnecting the power (watts) between devices. Such complete matching can be done conveniently by adding resistance to the circuits. Figures 2.1a and 2.1b show the use of resistors to match impedances. In Figure 2.1a the impedance of the source is higher than that of the load. In this case the appropriate resistance has been added to the circuit in series. **In series** means that the voltage has only one path to follow through the circuit. If the reverse were true and the impedance of the load were higher than that of the source, as in Figure 2.1b, the resistance would be added in parallel. **In parallel** means that there is more than one path for the voltage to follow through the circuit.

When you are concerned with interconnecting voltage (rather than power) between systems, as you frequently will be in the speech and hearing sciences, it is really not necessary to have a perfect match between the impedances. So long as the impedance of the load (the downstream piece of equipment) is not

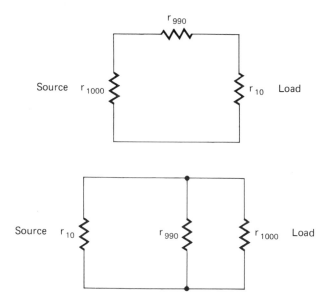

Figure 2.1 Circuit showing source impedance higher than load impedance and in series resistor added to match impedance and circuit showing load impedance higher than source impedance and in parallel resistor added to match impedance.

so low as to seriously alter the operating characteristics of the source (the upstream piece of equipment), a satisfactory connection will have been made. However, you can inadvertently lower the impedance of the load by making a connection to another instrument. Whenever a load is connected across the output terminals of a source, the load is said to be in parallel with the source. Assume, for example, that a small amplifier (i.e., source) with an output impedance of 10 Ω is connected to a loudspeaker (load) with an impedance of 10 Ω as in Figure 2.2. In this example the impedances are in parallel, and they total 5 Ω. Substituting into Equation 2.1, you get

$$10 \times 10/(10 + 10) = 5.$$

Assuming that the source was designed to operate into 10 Ω and to output maximum power into 10 W, the intent of the designer would not be met and you would have a 50% loss of signal strength. To correct this situation, you must increase the input impedance of the load. If the load impedance is higher than the source impedance, the transfer of energy is much more efficient than if the reverse is true. So, as a general rule of thumb when you connect equipment, take care that the load impedance is higher than that of the source. This will minimize or prevent the load from consuming all the energy of the source and thus distorting the transduction process.

GROUNDING OF EQUIPMENT

As was discussed in Chapter 1, grounding means making sure that the electrical supply to the equipment has been provided a path to earth. This ensures that stray current that may result from a short will be shunted to earth and not pass through the body of some unlucky person.

When you are dealing with only a few pieces of equipment, proper grounding is normally not too difficult. When large numbers of instruments are sequenced together, however, the problem can become major. All the

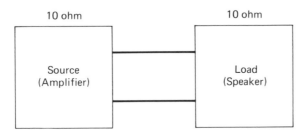

Figure 2.2 Circuit showing mismatched impedance.

power cords of the instruments should be of the three-prong type, and all three of the prongs should be plugged into a grounded outlet. The third, or round, prong connects the equipment to the earth through the central ground in the building. This ensures that each piece of equipment is grounded, and it reduces the possibility of hum resulting from 60-Hz power line frequency and possible shock hazard.

PATCH CORDS

One of the universally accepted "truths" in the laboratory or the clinic is that when you want to connect two instruments together, you will find their input/output connectors to be different. This can be a frustrating experience unless you have access to a variety of patch cords and connector adapters. Figure 2.3 shows several such adapters.

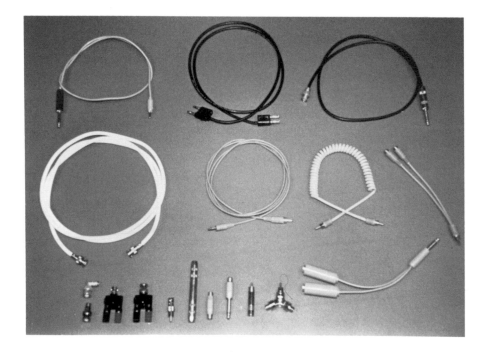

Figure 2.3 An assortment of patch cords and adapters (from left, top row) phono to tape, banana to banana, BNC to phono (2nd row) BNC to BNC, miniphone to tape, tape to tape, tape "Y" adapter (3rd row) BNC right angle, BNC to tape, female BNC to banana, male BNC to banana, male tape to phono plug, male phono to tape plug, tape splitter, phone "Y" adapter.

With a bit of ingenuity and some patience, you can usually put together several cords or connectors in such a fashion that the proper terminal will appear (sometimes as if by magic) on both ends of the patch cord. One word of caution about these cords and adapters is that in some cases they are designed for stereo transmission. This is particularly true of certain $\frac{1}{4}$ in. phone plugs and receptacles. The connection of a stereo phone plug to a mono input receptacle can result in a short that will prevent the transfer of any signal. It is generally easy to tell the stereo from the mono plug because the stereo plug has an extra section. Both types of plugs are shown in Figure 2.6. Certain types of connectors are used more often than others on some pieces of equipment. For example, the BNC connectors shown in Figure 2.3 are frequently used on oscilloscopes and filters. They have the advantage that they will not slip off the equipment since they twist on and lock. The so-called RCA connectors are almost always found on patch cords destined to be used on tape recorders and other types of audio and video equipment. Banana plugs are found frequently in the laboratory since it is quite easy to stack them together, thus allowing for the quick connection and disconnection of several pieces of equipment to the same input or output.

SOLDERING

Occasionally, no matter how diligent and inventive the clinician or investigator, no appropriate patch cord will be found, which means that the proper connecting cord must either be purchased or manufactured on the spot. The purchase of specially made patch cords is a time-consuming and expensive task. If the parts are available, it is far more efficient in terms of time and money for you to fabricate the connecting cord yourself. To do so, you must have some knowledge of a connecting technique known as soldering.

Soldering is not a difficult skill, and with some practice almost anyone can do it. **Solder** is metal that is usually a mixture of tin and lead used to bond two pieces of metal together. Solder will easily bond copper, iron, steel, tin, gold, and silver together. It can be purchased at just about any electronics or hardware store at very low cost. When choosing solder, look on the package or roll for numbers such as 50/50 or 60/40. These numbers indicate respectively the percentage of tin and lead in the solder. The project itself usually dictates the tin/lead content of the solder you should buy. For most purposes involving the soldering of wire or electronic components, a solder with a low melting point, such as 60/40, should be used. Figure 2.4 shows the tools that are required to do an adequate soldering job in the clinic or lab.

Before beginning to solder the patch cord together, cut the wire to the proper length. It is advisable to cut the wire a bit longer than necessary so that if you make a mistake, you can make a new start without throwing away the

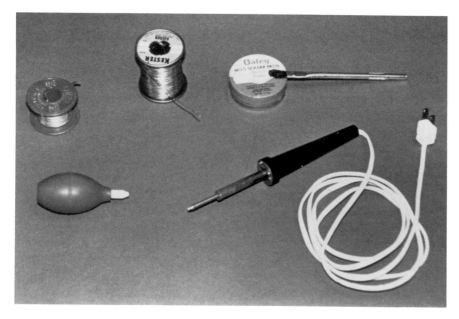

Figure 2.4 Common tools needed for soldering (from bottom left): solder "sucker," large diameter solder, small diameter solder, paste flux with brush, pencil style soldering iron.

length of wire. Single conductor **coaxial cable** is the best to use for a patch cord. Figure 2.5 shows this type of wire in cross section and from a side view. Notice that it has an outer covering (the insulation) with the next layer being a fine mesh of copper (the shielding). The shielding is followed by additional insulation containing the conductor. The shielding on this type of wire helps to prevent the pickup of stray electrical current; that benefit outweighs any cost savings you may have gained by buying any other type of wire for this purpose.

The next step is to select the type of connector or connectors that you wish to use to terminate the patch cord. This choice is dictated by the connections you need to make. When you take the connector apart, as you must to solder it to the wire, you will notice that it has at least two places for the wire to be connected (three if it is a stereo connector). Figure 2.6 shows a popular connector called a $\frac{1}{4}$ in. "male" phone plug. If you took it apart you would see that the male plug has a long and a short prong for connection to the wire. Typically, the central conductor of the cable is connected to the short prong and the shielding is connected to the longer prong.

Once you have taken the connectors apart, inspect them to see if any part of them (such as the plastic sleeve) must go over the wire when the job is finished. If this is the case, slip those parts on over the wire before beginning; otherwise after the job is done there will be no way to get them on—which can be

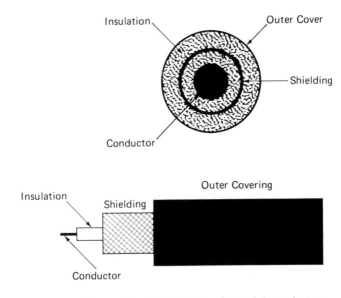

Figure 2.5 Components of coaxial conductor.

disturbing because the connections must be taken apart and begun again. Once you have exposed the internal portions of the connectors, make sure that they are clean and free of any oxidation. If not, you can clean them with a wire brush before you begin to solder. Solder will not stick to dirty metal no matter how hot you make the solder. A solution called **flux**, made for cleaning metals for soldering, can be purchased to aid in this cleaning step. Be careful with the flux; it contains acid.

Once the soldering iron is hot, you can clean the tip of the iron with flux. If the tip is very dirty or has an accumulation of old solder built up on it, you may have to take the wire brush or sandpaper to it. If the tip must be cleaned down to bare metal, it should be "tinned" before you begin to solder. Tinning is accomplished by melting solder on the tip and then wiping the tip on a rag or a slightly wet sponge, which leaves a thin covering of solder on the tip.

You must now remove the covering on the wire so that the wire is bared (remove just enough to make an attachment possible). Tin the exposed ends of the wire and the attachment points on the connector to facilitate the eventual connection. Once the tinning is done, join the wire and the connector, apply more solder, and hold the heat to the joint until the solder all melts together. Now remove the heat. The solder will cool (it becomes dull looking) and will complete the connection.

The final step in the process is to make certain that there has been no interconnection (electrical short) between the conductor and the shielding anywhere in the connection process. This is called a continuity check and is

Figure 2.6 Single-conductor (mono) $\frac{1}{4}$ in. phone plug (r) and two-conductor (stereo) $\frac{1}{4}$ in. phone plug.

accomplished with the use of a volt/ohm meter. Set the meter to measure ohms (resistance), and place one lead of the meter on the portion of the connector that was attached to the central conductor of the wire and the other lead on the portion of the connector attached to the shielding on the opposite end of the patch cord. If the two sides of the connection have been kept separate (as they should have been), the meter will not deflect. Now, without moving the lead from one end of the wire, move the lead on the other end to the corresponding portion of that connector. Now the meter should deflect because there should be continuity under that circumstance. If your patch cord passes these tests, it is ready to be used. (See Table 2.1 for tips on soldering.)

LABORATORY EXERCISES

Exercise One

This is a simple identification exercise that will reinforce what you have read about inputs, outputs, and connectors. Find a tape recorder. Any type will do, although if you can find a reel-to-reel recorder use that instead of a cassette recorder.

TABLE 2.1
Tips on Soldering

Problem	Cause	Solution
Metals don't fuse	Surface dirt	All foreign substances, dirt, oil corrosion, must be removed before soldering. Use steel wool, wire brush, or emery cloth to clean metal surfaces.
Metals don't fuse	Improper use of flux	Spread a thin coat of flux over all surfaces to be joined. This removes surface oxides and helps solder flow.
Metals don't fuse	Cold solder	If solder melts but connection remains loose, heat may have been applied directly to solder. Always apply heat to metal so that metal can melt solder.
Heated metal doesn't melt solder	Heat is dissipating	Large pieces of metal tend to draw heat away from solder connection. Increase the quantity of heat by using a higher wattage soldering iron or by using a soldering torch.
Solder evaporates	Too much heat	If solder smokes and evaporates, the metal is too hot. Normally entire heating/soldering process should be completed in under one minute.
Solder connection breaks	Inadequate mechanical connection	Even a good solder connection will break under torsion stress. Twist, screw, revit, or use other mechanical means before soldering. Then use solder to fuse the connection.
Heat damages adjacent components or connections	Heat sink needed	Grip wire or metal leads with rubber-handled pliers between the solder point and the area to be protected. On large jobs, such as plumbing fittings, use a wet rag instead of pliers. (Do not grasp rag while soldering.)

Note. From *The Family Handyman Magazine,* November 1981, p. 110. Copyright 1981 by Webb Publishing Co. Reprinted with permission.

Step 1. Identify the "line" and the "mic" inputs.

Step 2. Identify the output connectors or jacks.

Step 3. Decide what types of connectors or patch cords must be used in order to connect to these inputs and outputs.

Exercise Two

In this exercise, you will actually make the equipment work for you. Find a small amplifier. If you have no idea what an amplifier looks like at this stage, ask your instructor. Have the operations manual for the amplifier handy while you perform this experiment. See the equipment flowchart, Figure 2.7, for additional help.

> **Step 1.** Identify the microphone input to the amplifier, determine the need for any special connectors or adapters, and plug the microphone into the amplifier.
>
> **Step 2.** Identify the outputs of the amplifier, determine the need for special connectors or adapters, and attach either an earphone or a loudspeaker to the amplifier output.
>
> **Step 3.** Identify the volume control on the amplifier.
>
> **Step 4.** While adjusting the volume-control up and down, speak into the microphone and see if your amplified voice is heard.
>
> **Step 5.** If you do not hear any amplification, check to be sure that you have the proper input/output connections, that you have plugged in and turned on the amplifier, that you have a working microphone, and that you have turned the volume control in the proper direction.

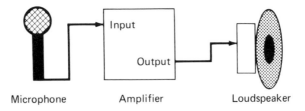

Figure 2.7 Equipment flowchart for Exercise Two.

KEY TERMS

coaxial cable   in parallel
flux   in series
impedance   solder
impedance matching

SUGGESTED READINGS

Curtis, Jack F., and Martin C. Schultz. *Basic Laboratory Instrumentation for Speech and Hearing*. Boston: Little, Brown, 1986.

Dawson, William L. *Instrumentation in the Speech Clinic*. Danville, IL: Interstate Printers & Publishers, 1973.

Hicks, M. Robert, Jerald R. Schenken, and Mary Ann Steinrauf. *Laboratory Instrumentation*, edited by C.A. McWhorter; Hagerstown, MD: Harper & Row, 1980.

Strong, Peter. *Biophysical Measurement*. Beaverton, OR: Tektronix, 1970.

Varoba, Barry. *Experiments in the Hearing and Speech Sciences*. Eden Prairie, MN: Starkey Laboratories, 1978.

CHAPTER 3

Transducers

A fundamental aspect of both clinical and experimental work in the speech and hearing sciences is that the sounds and movements that are important to us are much too minute to be measured by direct observation. Consequently, there must be a way to convert the original sound or movement into another more observable form. This process is known as **transduction** and is performed by a transducer.

A **transducer** is simply a device that is capable of changing one form of energy (e.g., sound) into some other form of energy (e.g., electrical current). It is important that the transducer do its job of conversion so that the altered form of the original energy is proportionately related to the original signal. Without this constant proportion, the new form of the signal would bear no understandable relationship to the original form.

In the speech and hearing clinic or lab, the most commonly used transducers are microphones and loudspeakers. There are other types of transducers, however, that are useful for many measurement tasks. They are of two broad classes: resistive transducers and displacement transducers.

RESISTIVE TRANSDUCERS

The operating principle of the **resistive transducer** is that its resistance to the flow of electrical current changes in proportion to the change in the physical quantity being measured. This change in resistance is then reflected in the changing flow of electricity in some additional part of the system. Figure 3.1 shows a circuit known as a **Wheatstone bridge**, which is popular for most resistive transducers and allows for the transduction of very small changes in physical energy. The circuit contains a constant power supply and four resistors. The resistors are so balanced that when the transducer is at rest the voltage across the output is zero. If you place a meter between the output terminals, its needle will point to zero. If you activate the transducer by applying physical energy one or more of the resistors will change in value, thus causing the bridge to become unbalanced and voltage to flow. If you now place a meter between the terminals of the system, its needle will be deflected in one direction or the other. The extent of the deflection will be in proportion to the strength of the original physical signal.

An example of a resistive transducer is a **thermistor**, which measures temperature change. A metal that is sensitive to changes in temperature can be used as the resistance part of the circuit. As temperature rises and falls, the resistance of the metal changes, and consequently the amount of current that is allowed to pass through the transducer rises and falls. By careful calibration, these alterations in resistance can be easily converted to changes in temperature.

DISPLACEMENT TRANSDUCERS

A **displacement transducer** can convert either linear or angular displacement into an electrical output. One of its most common forms is the **strain gauge** circuit shown in Figure 3.2. A very fine wire is glued to a surface such as paper or some other bendable or stretchable material, which is then placed on the physical system to be measured. When the system to be measured bends, it causes the backing material of the strain gauge to bend, thus causing the wire

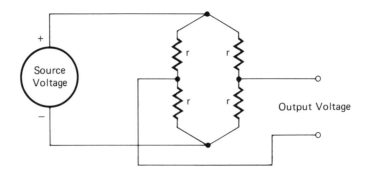

Figure 3.1 Wheatstone bridge circuit.

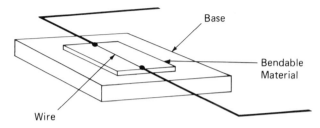

Figure 3.2 Structure of typical strain gauge.

to stretch. When the wire stretches, its resistance goes up and the flow of current goes down. Thus, in the same manner as described for the resistance transducer, the alteration in current flowing through the transducer represents the linear or angular displacement of the object being measured. Because they can be made very small, strain gauges are often used in the transduction of movements associated with speech musculature. For instance, a strain gauge can be placed on the upper lip to measure the type and amount of movement associated with the production of plosive speech sounds.

Another example of the displacement transducer operates on the principle of the **piezoelectric effect**. When two solid crystals are fastened together face to face and then distorted, a small electrical charge is given off. This charge is in proportion to the original displacement. Once the small charge is amplified, it can then be used as a measure of the original physical force. The principal advantage of this type of displacement transducer is that no initial energy source is required; the crystals supply their own. The piezoelectric transducer is used in some microphone construction.

Accelerometers are another means for transducing motion. Figure 3.3 shows the construction of a basic accelerometer, which consists of a suspended mass with a coil attached to it. The relative movement of this mass that is caused by the original force causes the coil to move over a permanent magnet. When the coil moves around the magnet, induced current that is in proportion to the degree of acceleration of the mass flows to the remainder of the transducer circuit. Accelerometers can be useful devices in the measurement of such small movement as that of the jaw during speech.

TRANSDUCER CHARACTERISTICS

Transducers have several characteristics that are desirable and contribute to the overall fidelity and sensitivity of the device. Because of its physical structure, a given transducer will have given impedance characteristics. Those impedance characteristics will then influence the manner in which that

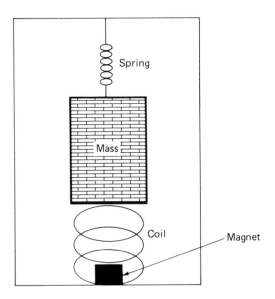

Figure 3.3   Structure of typical accelerometer (acceleration transducer).

transducer "transduces" the signal. Two different transducers therefore should not be expected to react similarly to the identical signal. Important character-istics to be discussed in the following sections are maximum amplitude linearity, minimal hysteresis, adequate frequency response, adequate sensitiv-ity, and minimal internal noise.

Maximum Amplitude Linearity

The signal that the transducer produces must be in proportion to the amplitude of the input signal. If it is not, you will get misleading measurements. Ideally, the linearity deviations of the typical transducer should not exceed 1% across the range of input values that are to be measured.

Minimal Hysteresis

Hysteresis is a measure of the ability of the transducer to produce an output that follows the input independently of direction of the change in input. A measurable difference at the output between continuous increases and contin-uous decreases in the input of the same signal are not wanted. As an example, a microphone should give the same voltage output for a constant intensity level frequency sweep whether that sweep is from low to high or high to low.

Adequate Frequency Response

For an effective transducer, the overall frequency response is equal to or greater than the varying frequencies of the waveform being measured. Keep these variations in mind when you choose a microphone or loudspeaker. The frequency spectrum of music is more demanding than that of the human voice. You do not need a microphone or loudspeaker with quality suitable for music for transduction of the voice.

Adequate Sensitivity

As with frequency response, the sensitivity of the transducer must be capable of following the amplitude fluctuations of the applied signal. The sensitivity range must be responsive to the smallest changes in the external signal as well as to the largest changes in the signal. Otherwise, the output amplitude will not be a faithful reproduction of the input amplitude. The general term **dynamic range** refers to these characteristics. Thus, the dynamic range of the transducer must equal or exceed the dynamic range of the applied signal.

Minimal Internal Noise

Virtually everything with an electrical current in it has some degree of internal noise. Even with the best of transducers, thermal noise (sound caused by the flow of electrons or heat in the system) may interfere with the lowest levels of the input signal. The point at which the signal being measured becomes contaminated or mixed with the internal noise is called the **noise floor**. Once the strength of the input signal falls below this level, you will not be able to see fluctuations of the signal. Instead, a rather random fluctuation that is not necessarily associated with the signal will occur. Removing the external input signal from the transducer and then measuring the output of the transducer will quickly yield the level of the noise floor. It should be obvious that the noise floor of the transducer should be below the lowest amplitude of the input signal.

Having reviewed these fundamental characteristics of a good transducer, let us turn to a discussion of several of the more common kinds of transducers that are in use in the speech and hearing clinic or laboratory.

MICROPHONES

Microphones are used in all sorts of recording in which the voice or some other sound-producing device must have its energy converted, or transduced, to an electrical waveform. All microphones have some mechanism that allows them

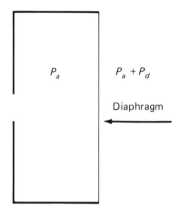

Figure 3.4 Pressure microphone schematic.

to be sensitive to changes in the pressure front of the acoustic waveform. The simplest of these mechanisms is a thin, flat piece of metal or plastic called a **diaphragm**. The pressure changes that occur in the sound medium are distributed across the face of the diaphragm, causing it to move.

Figure 3.4 shows a schematic diagram of a typical pressure microphone in which P_a equals standard atmospheric pressure, and P_d equals the pressure variation over or under the standard pressure provided by the wavefront. The diaphragm is in turn connected to the remainder of the transducer circuitry, and movements are then converted to voltage changes.

Some microphones are sensitive to pressure differences on either side of the diaphragm and are termed pressure gradient microphones. Figure 3.5 shows a simple view of this type of microphone. Again P_a equals atmospheric pressure, and P_d equals the pressure variation. Notice that the P_d factor is positive on one side and negative on the other, indicating pressure differences.

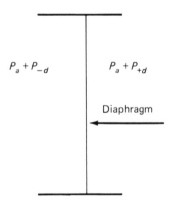

Figure 3.5 Pressure gradient microphone schematic.

Because the pressure gradient microphone responds best when there are opposing pressure differences on the two sides of the diaphragm, it is quite directional in operation. Because the pressure microphone is sensitive to any pressure variation, it is said to be omnidirectional. Figure 3.6 shows the pattern of sensitivity for both types of microphones. The plots seen in Figure 3.6 are usually referred to as "polar plots" because they show the sensitivity pattern of the microphone as the sound source is rotated about 360 degrees. Notice that the response pattern of the omnidirectional microphone (Figure 3.6a) is a good bit more symmetrical than that of the directional microphone (Figure 3.6b). The symmetry of the omnidirectional microphone shows that it responds almost equally well to sound coming to it from any direction.

Directional microphones have the advantage of not being as responsive to sounds that do not come to them from directly in front or from zero degrees of incidence. This property is useful for the reduction of background sounds when recording. Directional microphones have gained popularity in the construction of hearing aids. The wearer hears sounds coming from directly in front, but the sounds that are in the background are reduced — very helpful in understanding speech when several people are talking at the same time.

TYPES OF MICROPHONES

For most general types of recording and other routine uses of microphones, it is not very important what type of microphone you use. It is important to recognize, however, that different types of microphones have differing responses to sound; for certain applications the frequency response may be critical. As an example, recording speech for later analysis of its harmonic content requires the use of a microphone with a much wider frequency response than that used for the simple recording of a lecture. In addition, certain microphones produce larger output signals than others, which means that you must give careful consideration to the type of instrumentation with which the microphone is to be connected. For example, if the output of the microphone is very small, you may have to boost it with an amplifier before sending the output on to some other piece of equipment. In the remainder of this section we consider several types of microphones and discuss their construction and some of their advantages and disadvantages.

Crystal Microphones

Crystal microphones depend on the piezoelectric effect previously mentioned. The diaphragm is attached to the crystals in such a way that movement of the diaphragm causes the crystals to be bent, which causes a small electrical current to flow. Crystal microphones can be either omnidirectional or

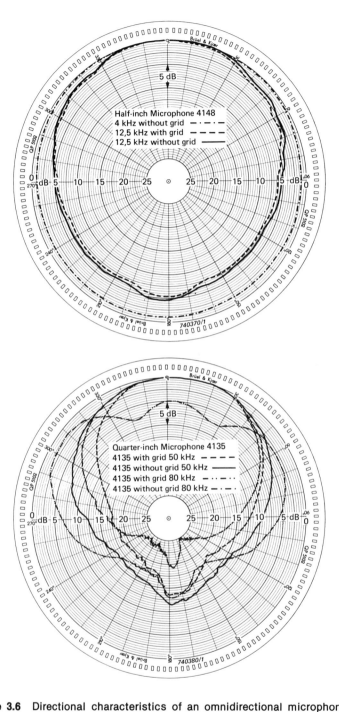

Figure 3.6 Directional characteristics of an omnidirectional microphone and a directional microphone. (Source: Courtesy Bruel & Kjaer Instruments, Inc., Marlborough, MA)

directional. Their frequency responses typically extend from approximately 80 Hz to about 6,500 Hz, making them useful for work involving recording the human voice. The major limitation of crystal microphones is that the voltage produced by the piezoelectric effect is very small and must be amplified soon after it leaves the microphone. Do not operate crystal microphones more than 16 to 20 m from the source of amplification. Otherwise you run the risk of also amplifying their internal noise. The dynamic range, sensitivity, and lack of distortion in these microphones are good. They tend to have good stability in their transduction properties provided that they are not operated in a humid environment, which alters the properties of the crystals.

Dynamic Microphones

Figure 3.7 shows the basic construction of the dynamic microphone. Attached to the diaphragm is a small coil of wire that is fitted around the core of a permanent magnet. The diaphragm movement causes the coil to be moved in and out of the magnetic field, altering that field, and current is caused to flow in the wire windings of the coil.

Because the dynamic microphone typically has a larger output voltage and lower internal noise level than does the crystal microphone, it can be operated at greater distances from the source of the amplification. Sensitivity, however, is not as good as that of the crystal microphone because of the increased mass of the system. Dynamic microphones are also sensitive to other electromagnetic sources such as neon lights, dimmer switches, and ungrounded power cables. If these things are unavoidable, the dynamic microphone is probably not the microphone of choice.

Condenser Microphones

Figure 3.8 shows the typical construction of the condenser microphone: a metal plate (diaphragm) and a back plate. These two surfaces are separated by

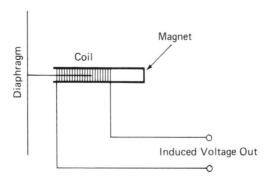

Figure 3.7   Diagram of dynamic microphone.

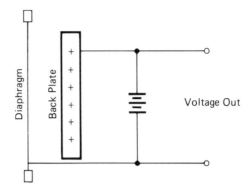

Figure 3.8 Diagram of a condenser microphone.

a very small distance and in effect form a capacitor. The capacitor is charged by a power supply—the **polarization voltage**. This voltage remains stable so long as the distance between the two plates (diaphragm and backplate) remains the same. Changes in air pressure produced by the sound cause the spacing between the two plates to change, thus producing changes in the charge of the capacitor. The variation in the charge causes current to flow in proportion to the movement of the diaphragm.

Although condenser microphones are usually rather expensive, they do conform to all of the "musts" for transducers. They are typically used in circumstances that require precise measurements. Calibration of audiometers is one such example (more will be said about this in Chapter 9). Condenser microphones usually have a very flat frequency response extending at least from 20 to 20,000 Hz. The actual frequency response depends on the construction of the microphone and the diameter of the diaphragm. Some $\frac{1}{4}$ in. or $\frac{1}{8}$ in. condenser microphones are capable of recording frequencies up into the range of 100,000 Hz. Such a microphone however, can cost in excess of $800. The major disadvantage of these microphones other than their cost is that the output impedance is high. With high impedance, the output voltage is dissipated rather rapidly over distance. Because of this, the typical condenser microphone has attached to it a small amplifier known as a **cathode follower**, which acts as a preamplifier, boosts the signal, and matches the impedance problems that occur. Even with this arrangement, the maximum distance over which a signal can be sent is about 3 m.

Electret Microphones

The electret microphone is a relative newcomer. Its construction is much the same as that of the condenser microphone. The principal difference is that instead of having a polarization voltage applied to it, it has a permanent charge that eliminates the need for an external charge. The cost of these microphones is typically far less than that of the condenser microphone, yet the performance is equivalent. Electret microphones can be made relatively small and can be clipped onto the clothes of the speaker, which can be helpful in creating a constant mouth-to-microphone distance. One drawback of electret microphones is that they are powered by a battery. If they are left plugged into another piece of equipment when they are not being used, the battery frequently will discharge. It is therefore important to make sure they are disconnected when they are not in use.

Probe Tube Microphones

The probe tube microphone is quite useful when it is necessary to make sound pressure level (SPL) measures within a closed or nearly closed cavity. If it were necessary, for example, to make sound pressure measures at the inside of the ear canal, a probe tube microphone would be a necessity.

Probe tube microphones consist of the usual transducer arrangements, but in addition, the diaphragm of the microphone is coupled to a length of tubing of very small diameter. The tubing is inserted into the cavity to be measured. Because lengths of tubing impose certain resonance characteristics of their own, the probe tube microphone is calibrated to the tube so that an appropriately flat frequency response can be obtained. One cannot alter the length of the tubing without also altering the calibration of the microphone. Figure 3.9 shows an example of one type of probe tube microphone.

Figure 3.10 shows the frequency response patterns of several of the microphones discussed in this section. You can see that there is quite a wide range of frequency response patterns. Notice that the dynamic and crystal microphones have a resonance peak at about 3,000 to 6,000 Hz that is absent in the condenser microphone. This is one reason why the condenser microphone is so useful in the calibration of other equipment. A broad and "flat" frequency response is a great advantage when very sensitive measures must be made and one wants to be sure that any deviations in the measured signal are caused by the signal's fluctuations and not those of the measuring device.

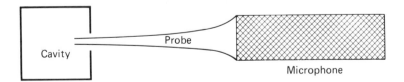

Figure 3.9   Diagram of a probe tube microphone. (Source: Etymotic Research, IL)

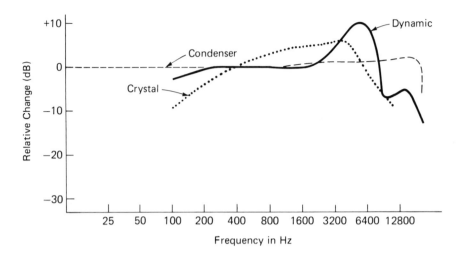

Figure 3.10 Frequency response of various types of microphones. (Source: *Instrumentation in the Hearing Sciences,* David L. McPherson. New York: Grune & Stratton, 1977, p. 107. Reprinted with permission.)

USING MICROPHONES

Use of Directional and Nondirectional Capabilities

The differences between omnidirectional and unidirectional microphones has already been discussed. Directional microphones are of some advantage when high levels of sound reproduction are necessary, but because of space limitations you must keep the distance between the microphone and the loudspeakers to a minimum. This condition frequently leads to feedback (squealing), but you can reduce or even eliminate the feedback by using a directional microphone. In addition, using a directional microphone where there is a high level of unwanted background noise usually improves the reception of the target signal. For example, suppose you wish to make a voice recording of one child in a noisy preschool setting. A nondirectional microphone would likely record all sounds in the room, but a directional microphone would minimize the recording of sounds distant from the child's mouth.

Angle of Incidence

Some microphones work best when the angle of incidence, the position of the source with the diaphragm, is something other than zero degrees (i.e., straight on). This is particularly true of certain condenser microphones that are used in the calibration of sound fields. It is important to remember that whenever a microphone is introduced into a sound field it will disturb that field. Microphones designed for sound field measures (so-called field microphones) automatically compensate for their presence in the field, and so can be used at zero degrees to the source. However, pressure microphones do not compensate for their own effects and are usually placed at 90 degrees to the sound source. If in doubt, always check the technical manuals that are supplied with most microphones.

Mouth-to-Microphone Distance

Mouth-to-microphone distance is especially important when you are making high-quality recordings of the human voice. Variations in the distance of the microphone from the mouth that may result from holding the microphone in your hand will appear as fluctuations in the amplitude of the voice in the final product. To minimize these variations, make recordings with a constant mouth-to-microphone distance by placing the microphone on a boom that is attached to a stand and then restraining the subject's head or, if possible, placing the microphone on a boom that you then attach directly to the subject's head. This technique also avoids the distracting noise that is caused by the overrecording of the plosive sounds of speech when the hand-held microphone is accidentally put too close to the subject's mouth. Although you will have to experiment with the best placement for a given microphone, a good starting mouth-to-microphone distance is about 15 cm (6 in.).

General Care of Microphones

It is obvious that you should avoid dropping a microphone or otherwise banging it about. A condenser microphone is especially easily damaged by bumping because the distance between its two plates is so small. If the microphone's diaphragm is accessible, avoid the temptation to touch it; the weight of the slightest fingerprint will change the calibration. In addition, should the diaphragm become covered with dirt or dust, take the greatest care in cleaning it. Remember that the thickness of the diaphragm may be only a few microns; it can be easily torn or punctured. If cleaning becomes necessary, it is best left to the factory or some other professional. Always return a microphone that has a storage case to the case when the mike is not in use. Keep a mike that does not have such a case in a dust-free drawer or cabinet.

LOUDSPEAKERS

Loudspeakers are essentially microphones in reverse. In theory at least, any microphone can be used as a loudspeaker, and sometimes they are. The inexpensive two-way intercom is a good example of this double duty. Depressing a switch that reverses the function of the loudspeaker within the intercom makes it function as a microphone or as a loudspeaker.

Most loudspeakers are dynamic. That is, they work on the moving coil principle just as does the magnetic microphone. The amplified voltage from the reproduction system is supplied to the coil of the magnet, which in turn causes the speaker diaphragm to move in and out, thus rarefying, or compressing, the air. Because loudspeakers must typically move a good deal of air, their diaphragms and coils are large. Some speakers work on the piezoelectric or electrostatic principle and tend to have the same characteristics as their microphone counterparts.

Loudspeaker design (i.e., diameter of diaphragm, size of coil, etc.) determines the frequency response of the system, and the needs for reproduction dictate what frequency response is needed. For instance, the frequency response needed to reproduce music is different from that needed for the reproduction of pure tones from an audiometer. Music contains many fast rise/fall time, short duration (transient) type signals. We understand that transients by definition are broad band spectrum signals and thus a speaker that has the capabilities to, for example, faithfully transduce piano music may need a frequency response out to 20,000 Hz or more. Pure tones, on the other hand, are typically long duration, relatively slow rise/fall time dignals that rarely exceed 8,000–10,000 Hz. Loudspeakers are usually contained within enclosures or placed behind baffles. These placements have an effect on the reproduction properties of the speaker, but the subject of loudspeaker enclosures is beyond the scope of this discussion. See the references at the end of this chapter for sources of further information.

Headphones

Headphones are a special adaptation of loudspeakers, being really nothing more than minispeakers contained within wearable enclosures. Some of these enclosures are intended to fit around the entire ear (circumaural) or to be worn over the ear (supraaural).

Headphones associated with music reproduction systems are often circumaural because this arrangement has the double advantage of improving the reproduction of the low frequencies as well as closing out distracting room noise. This type of headphone is also often used to test hearing, especially when the testing must be carried on under conditions of high noise level. As a clinical user of such headphones, you should also be aware that the possibility of stimulating the contralateral ear (i.e., acoustic crossover) is increased by the additional surface area of the head that these headphones cover. Consequently, you may need to consider a more conservative approach to the problem of contralateral masking.

Usually the headphone of choice for audiometry is the Telephonics TDH-50 or a variation thereof (TDH-39, TDH-49, etc.). These headphones are fitted into supraaural cushions (MX 41/AR) and typically have a flat frequency response over the frequency range necessary to test human hearing. The advantage of using this type of headphone over the circumaural phone is its ease of calibration. The supraaural cushion is designed to fit easily over the standard 6 cc coupler used in calibration (see Chapter 9).

Insert Phones

As the name implies, insert phones are designed to be inserted directly into the ear canal. The advantage of this design is that insert phones can be worn for long periods with comfort. Figure 3.11 shows an example of one such insert earphone. The driver mechanism is contained within a package remote from the entrance to the ear canal and is coupled to the ear canal by means of tubing and a soft sponge-rubber ear tip. The frequency response of the transducer is thus influenced by the diameter and the length of the acoustic coupling. The

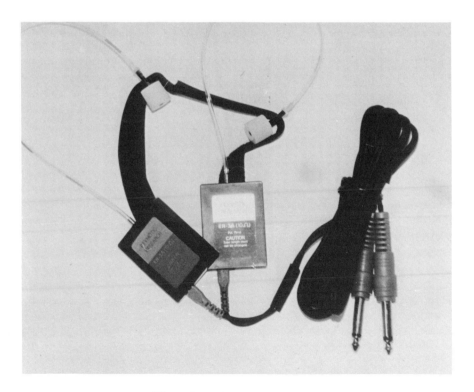

Figure 3.11 Insert earphones.

manufacturer has worked this proportion out, and it is therefore important that the tubing remain the same length.

Insert phones are being used in audiometry, particularly high-frequency audiometry, because of their excellent extended high-frequency response. In addition, because these earphones do not have the large surface area of the standard earphone, there is an attendant increase in interaural isolation. The practical importance of this for the clinician is that masking of the nontest ear during clinical evaluation may not be necessary in as many cases as usual. An increase in the acoustic isolation between the ears also means that higher levels of masking noise may be employed before the masking begins to cross back to the test ear (overmasking).

Insert phones can now be purchased with several different frequency response characteristics. For standard audiometry, responses that mimic the TDH-49 earphones are available. If the phones are to be used for certain types of human and animal research in which a very broad and flat frequency response is required, phones with these characteristics are also commercially available.

KEY TERMS

accelerometer	pressure microphone
cathode follower	polarization voltage
diaphragm	resistive transducer
displacement transducer	strain gauge
dynamic range	thermistor
hysteresis	transducer
noise floor	transduction
piezoelectric effect	Wheatstone bridge

SUGGESTED READINGS

Bruel & Kjaer Co. "Microphones Used as Sound Sources," *Technical Review,* No. 3. Cleveland, OH: Bruel & Kjaer Co., 1977.

Curtis, Jack F., and Martin C. Schultz. *Basic Laboratory Instrumentation for Speech and Hearing.* Boston: Little, Brown, 1986.

Khazan, Alexander D. *Transducers and Their Elements: Design and Application.* Englewood Cliffs, NJ: Prentice Hall, 1994.

McPherson, David L., and John W. Thatcher. *Instrumentation in the Hearing Sciences.* New York: Grune & Stratton, 1977.

Strong, Peter. *Biophysical Measurement.* Beaverton, OR: Tektronix, Inc., 1970.

CHAPTER 4

Digital Signal Processing

Computer-assisted acquisition and analysis of data have become so common-place that it is difficult to understand how we ever managed without them.

More often than not, when one thinks "computer," one thinks of a stand-alone device that is useful in the collection, manipulation, and storage of data. However, it is equally common for the computer to be linked with some other external laboratory or clinical device. Used in this manner, the computer serves both to control the external device as well as to collect and store the data acquired by that device. This chapter includes some basic concepts of digital signal processing and the ways the computer can be interfaced with other equipment to acquire and store information. Much basic information about the technical aspects of computers will be ignored because that is beyond our scope here. There are other, easily readable texts that discuss the technicalities of computer hardware and software. Refer to the "Suggested Readings" at the end of the chapter for books that will give you a basic understanding of how a computer works.

ANALOG AND DIGITAL DATA

Analog signals are best thought of as representations of the original physical event. They may be mechanical, like the movements of a joy stick, or they may be electrical, like the signals from the nervous system. The important part of the definition is that they are continuously varying events. If they are not already electrical, they must be converted by a transducer so that they may be used by our equipment. Digital waveforms are created when the original signal is represented as a series of digits or numbers. In its simplest form, this process consists of changing (i.e., digitizing) the waveform into a series of ones and zeros called a binary code. A **digital event** is an event composed of discrete or "step-like" values. The values are usually expressed as two voltage states.

An **analog event** is a physical event that can consist of any value. Examples include temperature, pressure, and velocity. Analog signals may be thought of as continuous, real-world events whereas digital signals are discrete, computer-world events. This binary code used by computers is usually a series of discrete electrical events consisting of two voltage levels. All information used by the computer must first be reduced to these two voltage levels. This process is called analog-to-digital (A/D) conversion and is discussed in the following paragraphs.

ANALOG-TO-DIGITAL (A/D) CONVERSION

Digitizer Resolution

Because they are digital devices, computers cannot operate directly on analog waveforms. Some method or mechanism must interface the computer to the analog event and convert that event to digital form. During the digitization process, the incoming waveform is sampled repetitively and the changing voltages are stored as numbers in the computer's memory. **Digitizer resolution** refers to the accuracy with which the A/D converter represents the changing amplitude information of the analog signal. The sensitivity of this process and the ultimate resolution of the incoming waveform is a function of the wordwidth of the A/D converter. Wordwidth refers to the number of **bits** (i.e., binary digits) contained in the digital word of the converter. For example, a 1-bit wordwidth provides only two steps of resolution: 0 and 1. A two-bit converter provides four steps of resolution: 00, 01, 10, and 11. Table 4.1 shows the wordwidth of several converters and the number of steps of resolution with each. The number of A/D steps increases as the wordwidth power of 2 changes. For example, $2^8 = 256$ steps.

Figure 4.1 shows the effect of two different A/D converters on the resolution of a simple waveform. You can see that the 1-bit converter with two A/D steps changes the signal into a square waveform, but the 2-bit Digitizer with its four steps of amplitude resolution creates a waveform that is much closer to the shape of the original.

Sampling Rate

Although digitizer resolution is an important issue in converting the amplitude of waveforms, an equally important issue is digitizer **sampling rate**. How fast

TABLE 4.1
Wordwidth of Several A/D Converters

Wordwidth (bits)	Number of A/D Steps
2	4
4	16
6	64
8	256
10	1,024
12	4,096
14	16,384
16	65,536

Note. From *Digital Signal Processing in Studies of Animal Acoustical Communication Including Human Species*, by R. O. Davis. *Computer Methods and Programs in Biomedicine, 23*(1986): 173. © Elsevier Science Publishing Company. Reprinted with permission.

must the incoming signal be sampled in order to accurately represent its frequency content? The answer is that the sampling rate must be at least two times the highest frequency in the signal. This is so because the Nyquist sampling theory tells us that in order to accurately preserve the information in

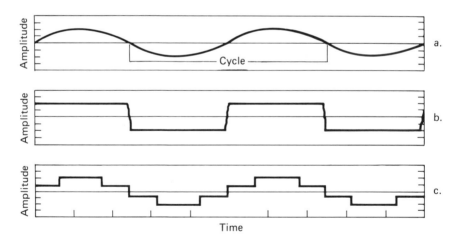

Figure 4.1 The effect of two different A/D converters on the resolution of the waveform: (a) analog waveform, (b) waveform obtained by digitizing analog waveform with 1-bit digitizer, (c) waveform obtained by digitizing analog waveform with 2-bit digitizer. (Source: "Digital Signal Processing in Studies of Animal Acoustical Communication Including Human Species," by R. O. Davis. *Computer Methods and Programs in Biomedicine, 23* (1986): 173. © Elsevier Science Publishing Company. Reprinted with permission.)

a signal, we must capture a minimum of two points per cycle. Figure 4.2a shows a simple 300 Hz sinusoid sampled at the rate of 10 kHz. At this rate, the smooth and continuous nature of the signal is well represented. Figure 4.2b shows the same signal sampled at 625 Hz, or just over twice the frequency of the signal. Now we see a different waveform but one in which the peaks still line up well with those of the higher sampling rate. Also notice that there appears to be some amplitude modulation of the waveform. This results from the interaction between the frequency of the original signal and that of the sampling rate. In Figure 4.2c we see the same waveform sampled at 312.5 Hz; the result is that neither the amplitude nor the frequency of the original signal is represented. This inaccurate representation of the signal is called **aliasing**, and it causes the original signal to be represented as being lower in frequency than it really is. Aliasing results when a signal is sampled at too low a rate relative to the highest frequency contained in the original. Sometimes an A/D converter comes equipped with an anti-aliasing filter to prevent these effects.

To summarize this discussion, choosing the appropriate A/D converter depends on the complexity of the amplitude characteristics and the frequency content of the signal to be converted. A waveform with a very complex amplitude function and high frequency components, such as a broad band masking noise, may call for a 16-bit converter and a sampling rate of 20,000 Hz, whereas a simpler waveform with lower frequency components, such as

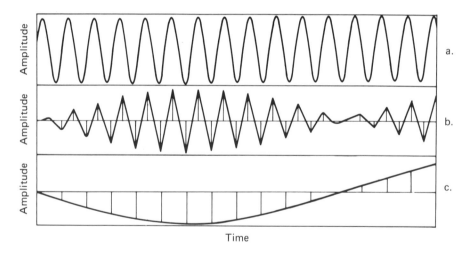

Figure 4.2 The effect of three different A/D conversion speeds on the resolution of the signal. (Source: "Digital Signal Processing in Studies of Animal Acoustical Communication Including Human Species," by R. O. Davis. *Computer Methods and Programs in Biomedicine, 23* (1986): 173. © Elsevier Science Publishing Company. Reprinted with permission.)

the rise and fall of respiration, may call for only a 6- or 8-bit converter with sampling rates of 500 to 1,000 Hz.

Digitizer Triggering

A side issue to consider when choosing a converter is whether it can be externally triggered. That is, does it have an input that allows the direct application of an external signal for a trigger? **Triggering** is a process of starting the capture of a signal at some specified moment in time. This is helpful in deciding when to start the digitization process. Otherwise, the converter must be programmed with software to begin its conversions at some specified point on the voltage rise of the incoming signal, or the process must be accomplished manually. Manual triggering of an A/D device is fraught with the same problems as discussed in Chapter 7 in connection with the manual triggering of oscilloscopes.

Serial and Parallel Input/Output

In some instances the design of the instrument that you wish to interface with your computer will be such that the data coming from that instrument will already be in digital form. In this case an A/D converter is not necessary. Computers have special inputs, called **ports**, that allow for the transfer of digital data between pieces of equipment. Ports come in either serial or parallel form. **Input** is when the computer receives information and **output** is when the computer sends information. In **serial input/output**, data comes into or goes out of the computer in a sequential fashion one bit at a time. In **parallel input/output**, data comes into or goes out of the computer by groups of bits. Many microcomputers can use both of these forms of input/output (I/0). Parallel interfaces are usually able to transmit data at a faster rate than the serial interface, but for many applications this would be unimportant. A common type of parallel interface is known as the Centronics port; the most common type of serial port is called an RS-232 interface. To use these I/0 arrangements, you must do some kind of software programming to let the computer know when the data transmission is to begin.

Multiplexing

Whether the input to the computer is by A/D converter or by some other I/0 arrangement, it is possible for the computer to sample data from several sources at the same time. This is called **multiplexing**. For example, the computer may be asked to sample data coming to it from electrodes attached to eight sites on the skull. This is accomplished by multiplexing. A circuit that precedes the A/D converter or input port samples the eight sites rapidly and continuously on a rotating basis. The computer keeps track of which site has been sampled at any given instant and stores that information to an appropriate place in memory. The primary advantage of multiplexing is that you do not need multiple A/D converters or multiple input ports.

SIGNAL AVERAGING

A powerful and useful technique for digital signal processing goes by the general name of **signal averaging**. This technique is useful when the signal you want to observe and measure is obscured by a background signal that is random and generally more intense than the signal of interest. One of the most common of these situations in the speech and hearing sciences is in the recording of auditory central nervous system activity from the scalp. Because auditory nervous system signals are weak and because the scalp is far removed from the site of the neuroelectric generators of the auditory system, the amplitude of the electrical voltages is small. There are, however, other biological (e.g., EKG and respiration) and nonbiological (e.g., 60-Hz line interference and radio stations) voltages on the scalp. These signals generally are much larger in amplitude than are the brain signals. By repeatedly sampling all these signals and averaging them over time, you can enhance the neural activity of interest and diminish the unwanted activity. The process works in the following manner.

Suppose that we have signals (e.g., electrical potentials from the brain) that occur with great reliability at the same time after the introduction of some external event (e.g., acoustic stimulation). Furthermore, suppose that these auditory potentials fluctuate in polarity over a certain period and that these fluctuations in polarity occur so that the positive and negative deflections always occur at the same interval after each repeated stimulation. If you were to sample such a signal through the process of A/D conversion in such a way that the converter began to sample at the onset of each stimulation, continued to sample over some specified interval, stored that sample to memory, and then sampled again, you would be signal averaging. The result of signal averaging such a waveform would be that the activity that is time-locked (i.e., always the same) to the stimulus would sum in computer memory and that which is random would cancel in memory.

In the past, signal averagers have been dedicated devices—that is, constructed to perform only the task of signal averaging. With the proliferation of desk-top computers, most manufacturers now rely on computer software to perform the averaging. Because of its versatility, the computer can be programmed to provide the stimulus to the listener, collect and average the incoming neuroelectric activity, store the activity for later reference, and provide for many kinds of off-line data manipulation. Although there are signal-averaging instruments available that cost many thousands of dollars, there are also those that cost little more than the price of a personal computer and the A/D converter. The list of options on these instruments goes down with the cost, but for many applications a long list of optional analysis routines is not important.

A/D CONVERSION OF DATA FROM OTHER DEVICES

Any instrument with the capabilities for outputting data to some other storage device such as an X–Y recorder or a strip chart recorder can be interfaced with a computer. If the instrument's design is such that it can be interfaced to the computer system via an RS-232 cable, it may be brought under the control of the computer with the proper software. If there is no provision for RS-232 interface (i.e., the instrument is an analog device) the instrument cannot easily be brought under computer control; however, the data from the instrument can be stored to the computer's memory or to a floppy disk.

Instruments with an output jack for connecting to a recording device have at that output the voltage change that represents the signal. Sometimes the wiring of this jack is labeled in the user's manual as the Y-axis output. This output lead can then be attached to the input of the A/D converter to supply the signal to be digitized. The remaining problems are (1) how to store the voltage fluctuations of the Y-axis output along with their corresponding X-axis (time) values, and (2) how to signal the A/D converter at the appropriate moment to begin conversion of the data.

The second problem is perhaps easier to solve than the first. When you buy an A/D converter, it makes good sense to buy one that is capable of being externally triggered — that is, somewhere on the converter there is an input at which an external signal can be applied. Because these trigger inputs tend to be highly sensitive, the initial rise in energy on the leading edge of the signal is often enough to start the conversion process. A better solution is actually to provide a trigger pulse (a brief rectangular waveform) at the leading edge of the data to be converted to ensure that each conversion interval will occur at precisely the same time as all the others. If the converter does not have the capability for external triggering, the process must be accomplished by software commands, which entails writing a special program.

The first problem, storage of time information along with amplitude information, presents more of a challenge. You must program the A/D converter to take samples of the incoming activity at selected times. You will need to write a program or buy one of the commercially available laboratory packages. These laboratory software packages usually have user-selectable time bases over which the incoming data are to be digitized. You then need only to know the period over which the information is to be collected.

With such a program, an A/D converter (with specifications appropriate for the signal to be digitized) and a personal computer, you can digitize and store data from a wide variety of instrumentation. In my own laboratory, this arrangement has been used for many years to make an old Apple II + computer work as a digital oscilloscope for recording a wide variety of signals, including the speech waveform. We can input speech to the system directly with a microphone, or we can input from tape. In addition, we have interfaced the system with a PM Pitch Analyzer (discussed in Chapter 5) to record and store fundamental frequency information. Also, at one time we interfaced the X–Y plotter output of a hard-wired signal averager (Nicolet 1070 series) with the Apple and stored averaged brainstem waveforms on floppy disks. The point is that with a little bit of knowledge one can store information from non-digital laboratory devices to computers when one does not have digital devices at the ready.

COMPUTER CONTROL OF EXTERNAL LABORATORY DEVICES

Although most of the discussion to this point has centered on using the computer to collect and store data, it is equally possible to use it to control other instrumentation. The basic challenge is to find an appropriate way for the digital language of the computer to be understood by the other real-world (non-digital) instrumentation. Recall that a computer "thinks" in terms of two logic levels (Logic 1 and Logic 0). These logic levels are usually represented by two voltage levels called **transistor-transistor-logic (TTL).** The actual voltage values differ depending on the computer system that you are using, but in general **Logic 0** is about 0.0 to 0.8 v and **Logic 1** is about 2.5 to 5.0 v. These two voltage values are available at the computer's serial/parallel I/O ports and may be used to govern the operation of the external device.

One of the simplest ways to control an external piece of analog laboratory instrumentation is through switch closure—that is, the flow of the 110 volt current needed to run the instrument is turned on or off by a switch activated by the TTL pulse sent by the computer. Figure 4.3 is a flowchart that shows the equipment for controlling the start of a tape recorder. Suppose that you wish to record some event off and on during the course of a night but do not wish to remain awake all during the experiment. You can program the computer to start and stop the recorder several times. As shown in Figure 4.3, the computer sends out a TTL pulse at the appropriate time to a relay (i.e., switch). The relay closes and allows the current to flow, thus causing the

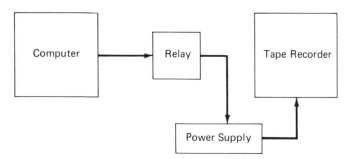

Figure 4.3 Computer control of a tape recorder.

recorder to run. At the appropriate time, the computer sends out another TTL pulse that this time causes the relay to open, thus stopping the recorder.

Speech and hearing laboratories frequently have a series of logic modules (e.g., timers, switches, function generators) such as the ones pictured in Figure 4.4. They are used to control the acquisition of data and the delivery of stimuli and are commercially available. They are extremely versatile because they can be "programmed" by interconnecting them into a certain series of events. They may or may not work on the same voltage values as does the computer system

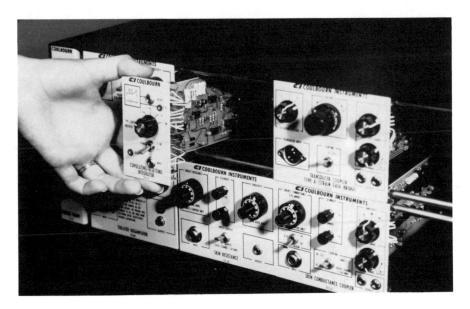

Figure 4.4 Logic modules for control of experiments. (Source: Courtesy Coulbourn Instruments, Lehigh Valley, PA)

being used. If they do not, you must interface the TTL pulse from the computer with the logic voltage used by the modules — an easy task. Figure 4.5 shows one such device — a 5 volt TTL Input Buffer. It receives the 5 volt TTL pulse from the computer and then sends out a 12 volt logic pulse that activates the module system. In this manner the computer (even a small computer) can be used to control the sequence of activities in a complicated experiment. In the more recent versions of this type of equipment, the control/data interchange between computer and external modules is accomplished by RS-232 connections and software programs.

Scientific equipment today is very different from the way it was even 5 or 10 years ago. A short trip down the aisles of the exhibit area of any large professional convention (e.g., the American Academy of Audiology [AAA]) reveals that most of today's sophisticated equipment has a microprocessor (i.e., computer) at its heart. Digital signal processing provides the speech and hearing clinician or scientist with a new range of methods for controlling data acquisition and storing and analyzing results of observations. Because of this, experimental questions can be asked today that would not have been thought of only a few years ago. Clinicians today can accomplish therapeutic tech-

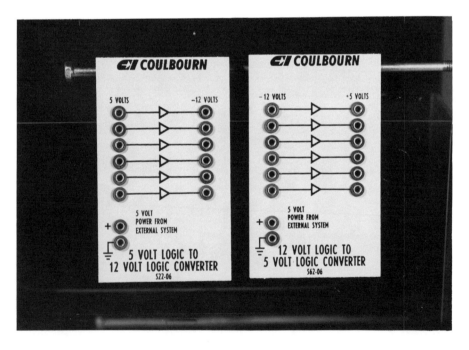

Figure 4.5 TTL buffer. (Source: Courtesy Coulbourn Instruments, Lehigh Valley, PA)

niques that would have been too complex to instigate only a short time ago. In short, computers and digital processors have given us a new look at our discipline.

KEY TERMS

aliasing	output
analog event	parallel input/output
bit	port
digital event	sampling rate
Digitizer resolution	serial input/output
input	signal averaging
Logic 0	transistor-transistor-logic (TTL)
Logic 1	triggering
multiplexing	

SUGGESTED READINGS

Coffron, James W. *The Apple Connection.* Berkeley, CA: Sybex, 1982.

Curtis, Jack F. *An Introduction to Microcomputers in Speech, Language, and Hearing.* Boston: Little, Brown, 1987.

Davis, R. 0. "Digital Signal Processing in Studies of Animal Acoustical Communication Including Human Speech." *Computer Methods and Programs in Biomedicine,* 23, 171–196, 1986.

Davis, R. 0. "The Personal Acoustics Lab (PAL): A Microcomputer Based System for Digital Signal Acquisition, Analysis, and Synthesis." *Computer Methods and Programs in Biomedicine,* 23, 199–210, 1986.

Decker, T. N. "Analog to Digital Conversion: It's not a Religious Experience." *The Hearing Journal,* May 1992.

Grossfeld, M. L., and C. A. Grossfeld. *Microcomputer Applications in Rehabilitation of Communication Disorders.* Rockville, MD: Aspen Publishers, 1986.

Silverman, Franklin H. *Microcomputers in Speech-Language Pathology and Audiology: A Primer.* Englewood Cliffs, NJ: Prentice-Hall, 1987.

Stearns, Samuel D., and Don R. Hush. *Digital Signal Analysis* (2nd ed.). Englewood Cliffs, NJ: Prentice Hall, 1990.

CHAPTER 5

Spectrum Analysis

The term **spectrum analysis** refers to a detailed observation of the individual parameters of some kind of signal. Although the spectrum of just about any signal can be analyzed, the speech pathologist or audiologist is typically interested in some acoustic event. For such events, the parameters of the spectrum that are important in an analysis are amplitude, frequency content, and phase. In the analysis process a signal can be displayed in two ways, or in what are sometimes referred to as "domains."

TIME DOMAIN

In the **time domain** the signal is pictured as a plot of amplitude versus time. So, for example, the sound of a very brief signal from an earphone might appear as in Figure 5.1. In this display we are able to observe how the amplitude (vertical axis) of the signal changes over time (horizontal axis) in the time domain, or the time spectrum. Although this is a useful display, it is of little help in visualizing the frequency makeup of the signal, although an observation of the periodicity of the signal in Figure 5.1 reveals some limited information about frequency. For instance, we can see that the periodicity in this signal changes from shorter to longer across the course of the event. This fact suggests to us that we are not observing a pure tone (a pure tone would have a constant period) and therefore that the event is made up of more than one frequency.

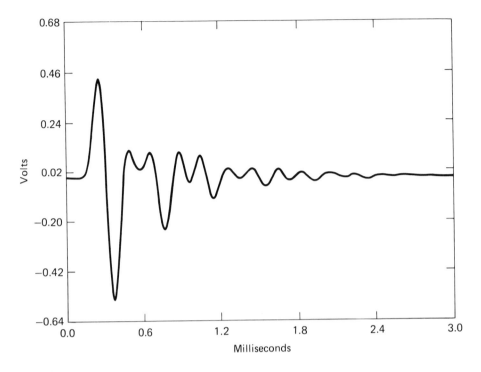

Figure 5.1 Example of the impulse response of an earphone in the time domain.

FREQUENCY DOMAIN

To gain a better understanding of the frequency content of such a signal, we turn to analysis in the **frequency domain,** or the Fourier spectrum. In this domain the signal can be displayed in two ways. First, the event can be plotted as amplitude against frequency, termed an **amplitude spectrum,** as in Figure 5.2. This figure shows us quite clearly that the signal is composed of several individual frequencies, each having different amplitudes.

The second way in which this signal can be displayed is as phase against frequency, or a **phase spectrum.** This kind of plot can be seen in Figure 5.3. In this particular example, we are able to see that most of the individual frequency components have the same phase relationships to the others. This might not be the case for a different example.

These plots can be generated because any signal can be expressed as the algebraic sum of its individual frequency and phase components. This is called the Fourier Transformation and is named for the French mathematician who developed the technique. Fourier analysis tells us that at any instant in time the

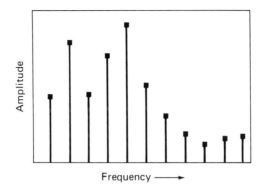

Figure 5.2 Example of an amplitude response in the frequency domain.

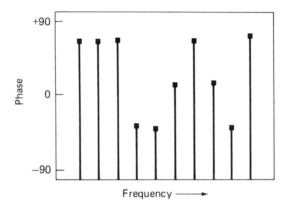

Figure 5.3 Example of a phase response in the frequency domain.

sum of the frequency and phase values will be equal to the amplitude and polarity of the original waveform.

Typically, when dealing with complex acoustic events such as speech, an analysis made in the frequency domain is much more informative than one made in the time domain. Time domain analysis, however, is much less costly, requiring nothing more than an oscilloscope, whereas frequency domain analysis requires some sort of spectrum analyzer.

REAL-TIME ANALYSIS

Spectrum analyzers can take the form of real hardware (e.g., a piece of instrumentation on a shelf dedicated to performing some type of analysis) or "virtual." Virtual spectrum analyzers are those that exist in the memory of a computer because of software that has been designed to allow them to analyze signals. Although computerized virtual systems are much more in evidence today than dedicated hardware, the dedicated systems still have their place. For example, many people agree that the computer systems still do not do a very good job of producing easily readable spectrograms. In the following paragraphs, several hardware systems will be discussed and used as examples so that the reader may fully understand the processes that are automated in computer systems.

In general, spectrum analyzers are designed to sample the spectrum of a signal with very narrow analog or digital band pass filters. Most of the present-day analyzers are digital and produce the analysis very rapidly. In fact, some analyzers are able to accomplish the process in "real time." That is, in a **real time analysis**, the complex waveform is converted to its narrow band component parts and is immediately displayed in a fashion that allows for easy visualization of the relationships between the amplitudes, frequencies, and the phases of the signal components. Figure 5.4 shows one such dedicated real-time spectrum analyzer.

Real-time analyzers are very nice in the sense of immediate images of the

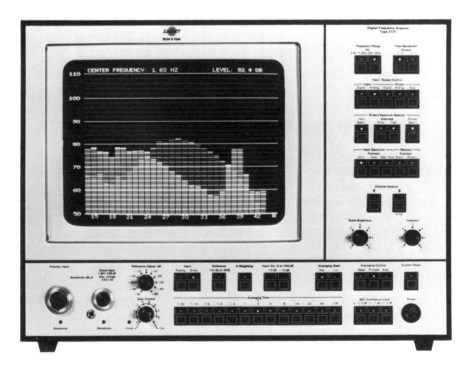

Figure 5.4 Real-time spectrum analyzer. (Source: Courtesy Bruel & Kjaer Instruments, Inc., Marlborough, MA)

waveform—they are also very expensive. An alternative method is to use a computer-based system with a software **Fast Fourier Transform (FFT)** program. Although this is usually not a real-time display, computers produce the results of the analysis quickly. Fast Fourier Transform programs are available for a wide variety of computers, including the IBM and the MacIntosh. With such systems, you can digitize a certain section of a waveform and then display it in a number of ways. You can even take pieces of the signal and rearrange them. This is useful for "tailor-making" certain types of speech stimuli.

Figure 5.5 shows time domain and frequency domain displays of the same waveform as might be produced by a desktop computer system. In addition to displays of the total waveform, you can, by recalling certain digital coordinates, listen to and display very small sections of the total. One compelling aspect of this kind of system is the ability to make recordings and store them on a magnetic medium (e.g., floppy disk). Such a system, for example, could be used to make and store spectrums of various types of masking noises or of signals transduced through various hearing aids. The system could also be used to monitor therapy by making and storing sequential samples of the vocal output of a patient.

SPEECH SPECTRUM ANALYSIS

One of the earliest efforts at creating an instrument to perform spectrum analysis in real time was that of the Bell Telephone Labs in the 1930s where scientists were trying to create an instrument that would display speech for the hard of hearing and deaf in such a manner that it could be used as a teaching tool. (For a historical review of this process, refer to Visible Speech by Potter R. K., G. Kopp, and H. Green, 1947). It was not long before the investigators discovered that the process took much too long to be used effectively as a teaching tool. However, after the rights to the instrument were sold to Kay Elemetrics, the instrument was offered for use as a research aid. This was perhaps one of the earliest speech spectrum analyzers that was ever offered at a price that was within the reach of departments of hearing and speech. As a result, Kay Elemetrics sold many of these instruments, and a good bit of the foundation work in speech science was performed using this workhorse spectrum analyzer. Figure 5.6 shows both an early and a more recent model of this device.

As originally developed by Kay Elemetrics, the device was called a "sonograph" rather than a "spectrograph" because the output was intended to be a sonogram, or display, of frequency plotted against time, with intensity indicated by the darkness of the tracings. Figure 5.7 shows an example of this display. For orientation, think of this illustration as a display of only the peak intensity information in the signal. Looking at a spectrogram is not unlike flying above and looking down on mountain peaks sticking up out of the

1000 Hz Triangular Wave

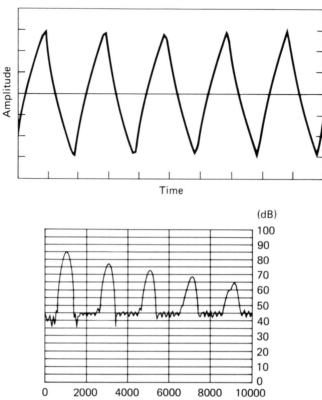

Time

(dB)

100
90
80
70
60
50
40
30
20
10
0

0   2000   4000   6000   8000   10000

Frequency (Hz)

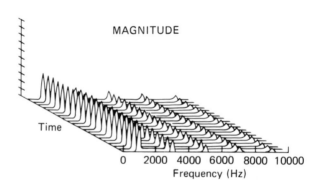

MAGNITUDE

Time

0   2000 4000 6000 8000 10000

Frequency (Hz)

Figure 5.5 Example of time and frequency domain printout from a software spectrum analysis system: (top to bottom) time domain display of triangular wave, frequency domain display of triangular wave, time/frequency/amplitude display of triangular wave.

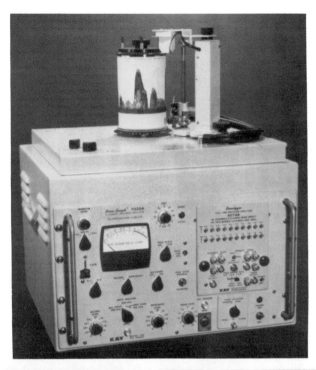

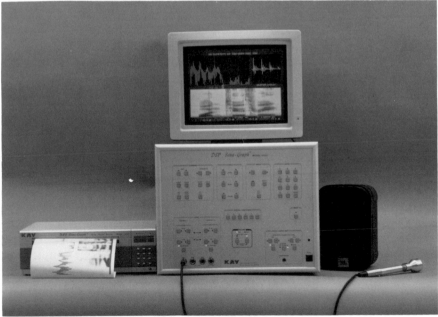

Figure 5.6 Example of early and later models of a speech spectrum analyzer: (a) an early model, (b) a later model. (Source: Courtesy Kay Elemetrics Corp., Pine Brook, NJ)

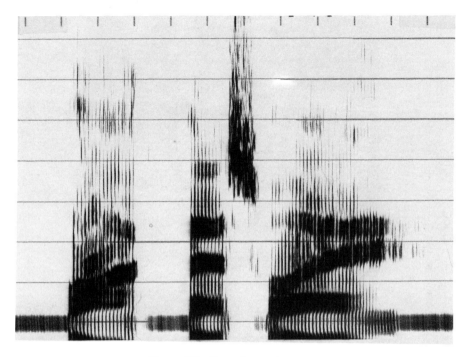

Figure 5.7 Speech spectrogram.

clouds. One knows intuitively that there are peaks that cannot be seen because they are below the level of the clouds just as the unseen peaks on the spectrogram are below the sensitivity level of the spectrograph.

The technology of the display is accomplished by curling heat-sensitive paper around a drum that rotates quite rapidly. Just above the level of the paper is an electrical stylus from which electricity arcs across to the drum. The strength of the transduced signal (electricity) produces lighter or darker burn marks on the paper. As the drum turns, the pen advances up the paper (on the short axis) delivering marks that represent the outputs of individual narrow band filters over successively higher and higher frequencies. The length of the sample is largely defined by the diameter of the rotating drum and consequently by the length (long axis) of the paper. The maximum time for the signal is about 2.5 sec. By making sequential recordings of 2.5-sec samples you could analyze quite a long sample — a rather tedious process, however.

The typical spectrograph uses at least two sets of narrow band filters for slightly different measurement routines. When the spectrograph is set to the narrowest mode (usually about 45 to 50 Hz), a spectrum 45 to 50 Hz wide is created that reveals the harmonic structure of the signal with fairly good detail. In the wide band mode (usually 300 Hz wide), individual harmonic content is lost but formant bands stand out more readily. Figure 5.8 shows the same signal analyzed in both ways. Although this is old technology, it is of some importance for the student to understand, as these instruments are still found in some laboratories and are useful for making high quality spectrograms.

THE SPECTROGRAM AND SPECTROGRAPH

Historically, the spectrograph has been thought of as a tool for analyzing the sounds of vocalization, whether human or otherwise. Within the instrument's limitations of analysis time and frequency sensitivity already discussed, the **spectrograph** can be used to analyze any acoustic event. When used in the conventional fashion, it can readily measure certain aspects of the voice. The following paragraphs provide you with a basic introduction to what can be measured as well as some suggestions for making measurements. It should be kept in mind that computer based systems accomplish all of the measurements detailed later in an automated fashion with the user making simple movements of the cursors and making observations of digital displays. Nevertheless, the knowledge gained from the following paragraphs will aid you in a basic understanding of spectrographic displays of the voice.

Fundamental Voice Frequency

The spectrogram in Figure 5.9 shows certain measurable aspects of the signal. At the very bottom of the spectrogram are the individual vertical striations that represent the fundamental frequency of the voice signal. The fundamental frequency (F_o, where F = formant) represents the lowest frequency produced by air flowing through the vocal folds. To calculate the fundamental frequency of the voice, you can use one of three methods.

Method One. This is the easiest method to use. Simply count the number of individual striations that appear on the wide band spectrogram in $\frac{1}{10}$ sec or 100 msec. Draw lines on the spectrogram 13 mm apart (100 msec), and then count the number of vertical striations that appear between the lines. Multiply this number by 10 (because you have measured the number of striations in 1/10 sec). For example, if there are 12 striations between the lines, the F_o would be 120 Hz. If a striation falls on your thin pencil line, you probably should count that in your total number of striations. In performing this technique, take several samples and find the mean value. If you have recorded voices with high fundamental frequencies, it may not be easy to count the individual striations because they will be very close together.

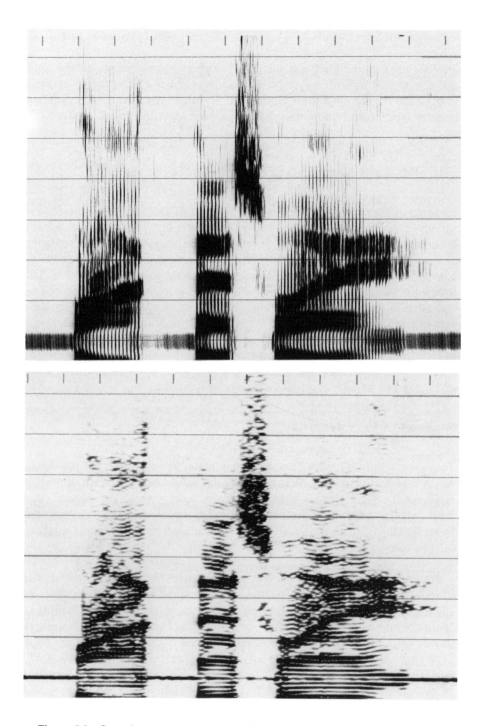

Figure 5.8 Speech spectrogram, (top) wide band and (bottom) narrow band.

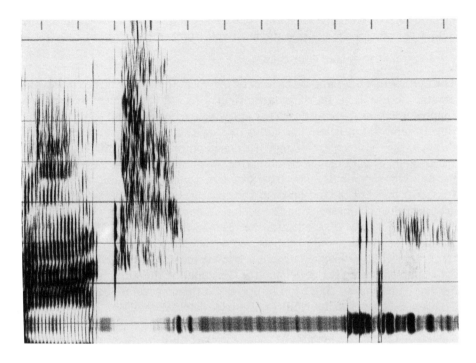

Figure 5.9 Speech spectrogram showing fundamental frequency markings along the bottom of the display.

Method Two. The next easiest method is to use the narrow band spectrogram of a sustained vowel or some other steady-state sample of vocalization. Simply count the number of horizontal lines (harmonics) you see between any two 1,000 Hz calibration lines on the spectrogram. Divide this number into 1,000 for the F_o value. For example, if there were five harmonics (horizontal lines) between the 1,000 and 2,000 Hz calibration lines, then the fundamental frequency would be 200 Hz (1,000/5).

Method Three. This method, like Method Two, requires the use of the narrow band spectrogram. Determine the fifth harmonic in any particular portion of the vocal pattern Ignoring any horizontal lines below the baseline and using a millimeter ruler, measure the distance from the top of the baseline to the midpoint of the fifth harmonic. It may help to draw a line through the harmonic before making the measurement. Take this millimeter distance value and multiply it by 72 Hz. Divide this value by 5, and the answer will be the fundamental. For example, let's say that the fifth harmonic is 7 mm from the baseline. Multiplying 7 by 72 gives 504, which when divided by 5 equals a fundamental of approximately 101 Hz. It is important to keep in mind that this method works for any harmonic chosen as long as the division of the millimeter value is made using the harmonic number chosen.

Formants and Formant Transition

The cavities that exist above the level of the vocal folds (i.e., throat, pharynx, mouth, etc.) act as a set of acoustic filters. As any filter does, these act to suppress the flow of acoustic energy at certain frequencies and to increase the flow at other frequencies. The bands of frequencies that are allowed to pass through these filters are termed formants and may be observed on the spectrogram as dark bands. By observing the placement of the individual dark bands of energy on the spectrogram, you can compute the approximate frequency limits of the formants in the vocal message. The formant groupings are especially informative where vowel information is concerned. For example, the second formant (F_2) indicates the resonance characteristics of the cavity between the tongue and the lips. With the tongue forward, F_2 rises in frequency; with the tongue farther back in the mouth, F_2 falls. The transition, for example between the vowel and the consonant in the word "box" in Figure 5.9 can be seen as a rising band of energy on the diagram in the locale of F_2. To estimate the formants, you can use one of two methods.

Method One. It is possible to get an estimate of the formant frequencies by measuring from both wide band and narrow band spectrograms. However, the wide band spectrogram is usually the better one with which to start. On the basis of your knowledge of where the formants should be located, draw a line through the middle of the thick, black bar. The center of the formant is usually close to the actual frequency of the formant. After you have drawn the line in the formant, then simply measure the distance in millimeters from the line in the formant to the baseline. Multiply this distance by 72 Hz, and the answer will be the formant frequency.

Method Two. Using a narrow band spectrogram and comparing the relative location of the formant from a wide band spectrogram trace, find the harmonic that appears the darkest. Two or more lines may look similar in darkness, so you may have to pick the one closest to the wide band marking. Draw a line near the point (harmonic or space between harmonics) that you think represents the formant frequency. Compute the distance measure in millimeters from the formant line to the top of the baseline, and then multiply this value by 72 Hz as in Method One. You can then compare this value with the one derived from Method One.

Duration of Speech Sounds and Voice Onset Time

Provided that the speech sounds are easily separable and discernibly different in depth of darkness, you can measure their relative distance from one another or their absolute length in millimeters and then convert to time by multiplying by a standard 7.7 (1 mm = 7.7 msec). For example, Figure 5.9 shows that the duration of the vowel in "box" takes approximately 192 msec to be completed. It also shows that the time between the production of the vowel and the onset of the final consonant is approximately 54 msec. The effects of coarticulation (i.e., the modifying effects of one sound on a preceding or succeeding sound) can be seen in Figure 5.10. In this example, the measurement of phoneme boundaries is a difficult but not impossible task.

Amplitude of Phonation

In addition to the information we have just discussed that can be provided by a spectrograph, you can also get some idea of the relative amplitudes of speech sounds over the changing course of the signal. The results are somewhat inaccurate because amplitude is not something that can easily be calculated on the spectrograph. Nevertheless, vowels, which contain the bulk of the acoustic energy in speech, normally appear as darker bands of energy than do consonants. Beyond this, there is little else that can be done to measure intensity objectively with this type of system.

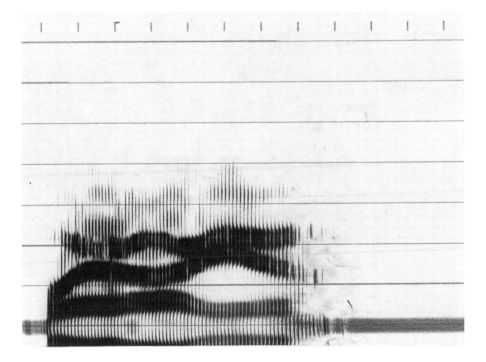

Figure 5.10   Spectrogram of the phrase, "Where are you?"

OTHER SPECTRAL ANALYSIS INSTRUMENTS

In addition to the spectrographs described earlier, there are other dedicated devices designed to measure one or more aspects of the speech spectrum. One of the simplest of these devices is the oscilloscope. As discussed in Chapter 7, the oscilloscope is useful for displaying the amplitude of a signal across some calibratable and constant time interval. By connecting a microphone to the inputs of an oscilloscope and producing a sustained vowel, you will observe a complex waveform that has a definite periodicity. Figure 5.11 shows the face of an oscilloscope set for a time display of 10 msec per division. The waveform on the scope is a sustained vowel [a]. At regular intervals of about one per division there is an amplitude peak. That peak represents the portion of the speech signal with the most amplitude and is the fundamental frequency. By calculating the distance between each of these peaks and converting to time, you can substitute into the formula, frequency (f) equals 1 divided by period (t), and derive the frequency value of the fundamental. For example, because we measured one peak every division and each division equaled about 10 msec (0.010 sec) of time, the fundamental is about 100 Hz (1/0.010 sec = 100 Hz).

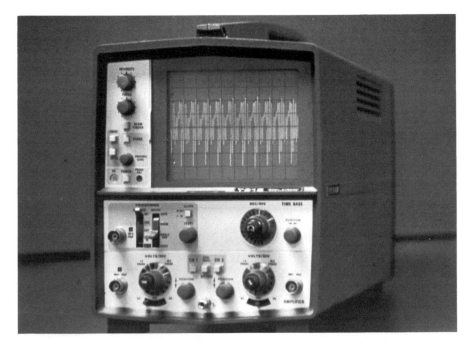

Figure 5.11 The waveform of the vowel [a] as displayed on the face of an oscilloscope set for 10 msec per division.

The oscilloscope may have limited measurement and storage routines for this work. For example, using a standard oscilloscope, it is impossible to see anything of the spectral content of a complex speech waveform. Because of this, there are several dedicated instruments for measuring fundamental frequency and other aspects of the speech waveform. These instruments are

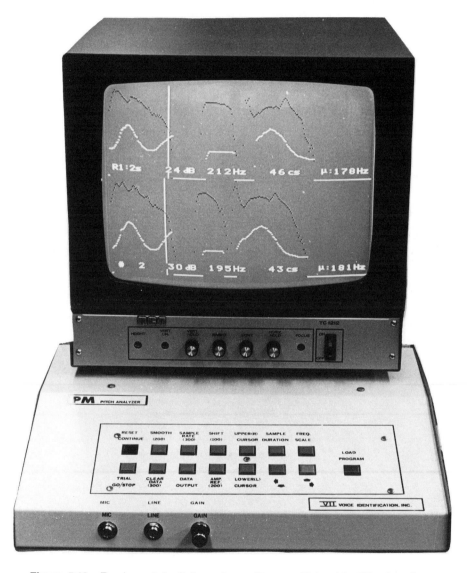

Figure 5.12 Fundamental pitch analyzer. (Source: Voice Identification, Inc., NJ)

termed *dedicated* because they are specifically designed to perform a limited number of tasks. Figure 5.12 shows one such system. This is a microprocessor-based system that is functional for measuring fundamental frequency and for measuring intensity in the fundamental frequency over a longer period than is usually possible on an oscilloscope. Once the sample is captured, certain descriptive information about it can be displayed on the CRT display. Figure 5.13 shows such a display of a fundamental frequency along with the accompanying descriptive data. In addition to the CRT display, the instrument may have an output that can be connected to an X–Y plotter or a strip chart recorder. These instruments can also be interfaced with a computer so that data can be stored to floppy disks. Additional discussions of interfacing these instruments with computers are in Chapter 4.

Finally, many software programs are currently available for use in measuring aspects of vocal activity. These programs are available for a variety of desktop computer systems and have differing capabilities. They are usually capable of displaying the time domain measure of the signal and of calculating various parameters of that signal. In addition, through the use of cursors,

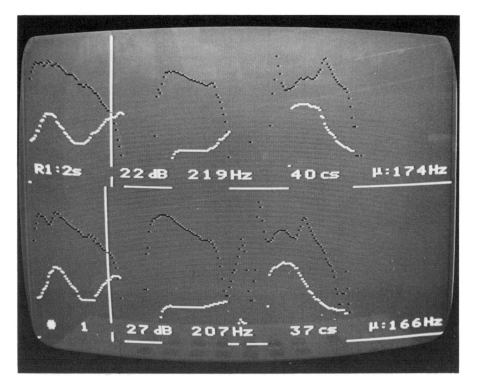

Figure 5.13   Fundamental pitch display. (Source: Voice Identification, Inc., NJ)

certain portions of the signal can be sectioned out for further analysis. For example, you may wish to know the time involved in the rise of energy in a voiced stop. By sectioning out just that brief part of a word and enlarging it, you can make further descriptive measurements. In addition, these computer-based systems also have options that allow for the spectral analysis of the signal, which is useful when you need information on more than the fundamental frequency. Although many modern software programs include such analysis capabilities as pitch tracking, the user must beware. The programs can be mislead by such things as esophageal speech, breathy voice, or unusually high or low fundamental frequencies. The most reliable methods still seem to be based on human examination of spectrograms or waveforms. Manual methods are typically used to check the veracity of automatic methods.

LABORATORY EXERCISE

This exercise is designed to help you visualize, on a prepared spectrogram, some of the measurements and concepts discussed in this chapter. The spectrogram shown in Figure 5.14 is of the phrase "Joe took father's shoe bench out" and was recorded by a male speaker. You will be unable to duplicate these measurements yourself because in the publication process the spectrogram has been reduced from its original size. However, after studying

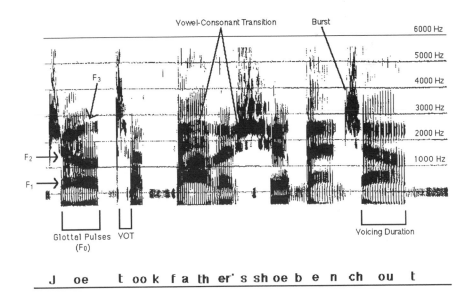

Figure 5.14 Sample spectrogram for the laboratory exercise.

this chapter and the spectrogram in this exercise, you may wish to make your own spectrogram on which you can practice these measurements.

Items You Should Observe

1. Find the markings F_1, F_2, and F_3. These indicate the first three formant regions (associated with vocal tract resonance). Notice that these regions can be observed only in those portions of the spectrogram that indicate vocalized information. Can you find other sections of the spectrogram where these formant regions can be seen?

2. The section marked "Glottal Pulses" encompasses the length of the voicing of the vowel portion of the word "Joe." It is in this section that you would make the measurements and calculations discussed in this chapter in order to find the fundamental frequency (F_o) of this speaker's voice.

3. The label "VOT" indicates the voice onset time, or the time between the release of the stop consonant and the first indication of the onset of the vowel. This time is also calculated according to the methods described earlier in this chapter.

4. The section marked "Vowel-Consonant Transition" indicates the region of energy on the spectrogram where the spectral modifying activity of the moving articulators is most noticeable. In general, this activity always occurs at about 1,000 to 3,000 Hz for most adult speakers.

5. The "Burst" denotes activity associated with the onset of a plosive speech sound and is seen in Figure 5.14 at the onset of the [ch] in the word "bench." Can you see another burst in this spectrogram?

6. Voicing duration can be calculated using the millisecond per millimeter calculations given earlier and applying them to sections of the spectrogram where glottal pulses can be easily seen.

7. Study the relationship between the vertical lines of the speech sound activity and the horizontal lines of the frequency calibration markers. This will help you to understand the spectral nature of speech and the differences that exist between vowels and consonants.

KEY TERMS

amplitude spectrum
Fast Fourier Transform (FFT)
formant
frequency domain
phase spectrum

real time analysis
spectrograph
spectrum
spectrum analysis
time domain

SUGGESTED READINGS

Baken, R. J. *Clinical Measurement of Speech and Voice*. San Diego, CA: College-Hill Press, 1987.

Borden, Gloria J. *Speech Science Primer*. Baltimore: Williams & Wilkins, 1980.

Bruel & Kjaer Application Notes. "Measurements of Harmonics, Difference Frequencies, and Intermodulation Distortion." Cleveland, OH: Bruel & Kjaer Co.

Curtis, Jack F., and Martin C. Schultz. *Basic Laboratory Instrumentation for Speech and Hearing*. Boston: Little, Brown, 1986.

Potter, R. K., G. Kopp, and H. Green. *Visible Speech*. New York: Van Nostrand Reinhold, 1947.

CHAPTER 6

Amplifiers, Attenuators, Mixers, and Filters

Sometimes signals are too weak and must be made stronger, sometimes they are too strong and must be reduced. Sometimes more than one signal must be sent to one input of an instrument and sometimes not all of the spectrum of the signal is important or wanted. These situations call for an understanding of very basic "workhorse" type instrumentation. In this chapter we will discuss amplifiers, attenuators, mixers, and filters, which are frequently used in the speech and hearing clinic or laboratory to condition and shape the signal and to route it to a particular place.

AMPLIFIERS

As the name implies, an **amplifier** is an instrument for increasing signal amplitude. One of the most basic of requirements of a good amplifier is that it should be able to increase the size of the signal without altering its characteristics. What comes out of the amplifier should be the same thing that went into it except that it should be larger. The amount of signal increase is referred to as the **gain** of the amplifier. Gain is equal to output minus input.

Although there are many different types of amplifiers for use in different applications, only preamplifiers, power amplifiers, and operational amplifiers will be discussed in this chapter. Although all of these types of amplifiers can frequently be seen as single, identifiable pieces of equipment, keep in mind that many pieces of laboratory equipment have within them one or more amplifiers that help accomplish the purpose of that instrument.

Preamplifiers

Preamplifiers belong to a special class of amplifiers designed to increase the voltage of the signal without providing for much of an increase in the current. Preamplifiers are usually used in applications in which some upstream transducer is producing a very small electrical signal that must be amplified before it can be sent on to the rest of the system. As an example, the cartridge in the tone arm of a phonograph produces only a tiny signal in the transduction of the record groove information to electrical signals. To increase this signal to a level that will be usable by the rest of the system, a preamplifier is placed after the cartridge. In this stage of the amplification process, there will frequently be associated mechanisms (in the form of tone controls) for controlling the frequency response of the preamplifier. These mechanisms are nothing more than filters and are discussed at greater length later in this chapter. Usually, the gain capabilities of the preamplifier are not all that great. If we wish to power any other pieces of equipment or perhaps another transducer such as a loudspeaker, we must use another kind of amplifier.

Power Amplifier

Recall from Chapter 1 that current multiplied by voltage results in watts and that watts are a measure of the power of the signal. If, for example, we wish to have our preamplified signal drive a loudspeaker, we must follow the preamplifier with a power amplifier. The **power amplifier** then takes the preamplified signal and boosts the current in the signal many times, thus providing the power necessary to make the loudspeaker work. Power amplifiers usually do not have any operator controls other than perhaps a gain control, but that is not important because the signal will have been conditioned by the preamplifier before it comes to the final amplification stage. Because of the large amounts of power that are generated by the power amplifier, it frequently gets very warm and must be placed so that this heat can be dissipated without damage to the amplifier or other components in the system.

Operational Amplifiers

Operational amplifiers are general-purpose amplifiers that are usually acquired as an integrated circuit that may contain one or more "op amps." It is readily apparent from looking at Figure 6.1 that the operational amplifier is

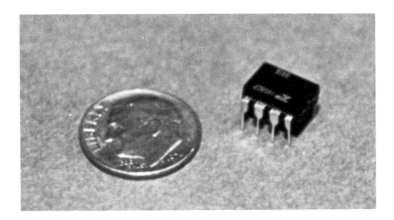

Figure 6.1 Integrated circuit operational amplifier compared to a dime.

very small. Because of its size, it can be incorporated into a variety of laboratory and clinical situations.

Figure 6.2 shows a schematic of an operational amplifier in its simplest form. The amplifier has two inputs, one that inverts the polarity of the signal and one that does not. If the signal is applied to the noninverting side, the output will be in phase with the input. If the signal is applied to the inverting side, it will be reversed in phase at the output. It can be seen that the output of the amplifier is connected to the input by a resistor, creating a feedback circuit between the output and the input. Depending on the type of electrical component that is in the feedback circuit, the amplifier can be made to perform such functions as simple amplification, integration (summation) of energy at the input over time, differentiation of changes in input energy over time, and adding (mixing) of inputs and subtracting of inputs. The op amp in Figure 6.2 is being used as a simple amplifier in which the degree of amplification is given by the ratio of the two resistors.

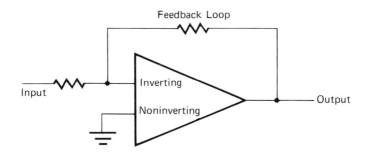

Figure 6.2 Circuit design of an operational amplifier.

Another common use for the op amp is shown in Figure 6.3. Here, signals from two different locations (i.e., places on the head) are applied to the two inputs. One of the inputs inverts the polarity of the signal, and the other does not. Because of this polarity inversion process, two signals with the same polarity at input will be canceled at the output (Figure 6.3a), and two signals with opposite polarity at input will be summed (amplified) at the output (Figure 6.3b). Through this process, the inverted signal and the noninverted signal are summed in the amplification process, and the result is seen at the output. Suppose now that the inputs of the amplifier were connected to electrodes coming from two locations on the head. Any signal that is common (i.e., has the same phase) at the two electrodes will be canceled, and any signal that is different will be amplified. This process is termed **differential amplification** and is frequently used in such applications as evoked potential recording (e.g., recording of brainwaves). Unwanted noise in an evoked potential recording should be common at both electrodes because the noise is rather uniformly spread over the head. However, brain activity is more localized and because of the placement of the two electrodes should not be in phase at the inputs to the amplifier. Thus the noise is canceled (or at least reduced), and the brain activity is enhanced. For more detailed explanations of operational amplifiers and amplifiers in general, refer to the Suggested Readings at the end of this chapter for further sources.

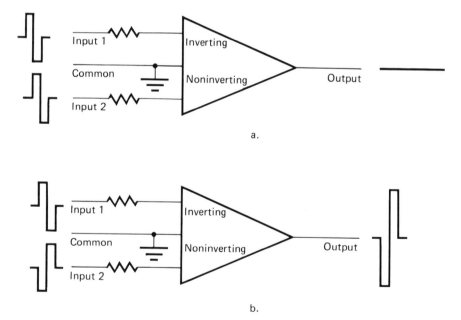

Figure 6.3 Circuits of a differential amplifier.

ATTENUATORS

Once the signal has been amplified, it must frequently then be reduced in value in discrete and calibratable steps. This activity calls for an attenuator. An **attenuator** is a device for dividing the input voltage by some predetermined value in order to reduce the voltage at the output. A **voltage divider** works on the principle of resistance and Ohm's Law. Ohm's Law states that the flow of electrons (i.e., current) is the product of the voltage divided by the resistance.

$$\text{Current (Q)} = \text{voltage (v)/resistance (r)} \qquad\qquad \text{Eq. 6.1}$$

The output voltage of a voltage divider equals the resistance ratio r_1/r_2 multiplied by the input voltage. Figure 6.4 shows a simple voltage divider and allows us to see how the voltage may be dropped to different levels with different values of the resistance ratio.

An attenuator, then, works on this principle of voltage division. The voltage division may be in discrete steps, in which case the attenuator is said to be a **step attenuator,** or in a continuous manner such as that provided by a volume control. Typically, the attenuator has a dial labeled in decibels (dB) of attenuation. The size of these steps of attenuation depends on the construction of the attenuator. Sometimes these steps are smaller than 1 dB, and for other applications they are 10 dB steps or larger. A 1 dB attenuator used in series with a 10 dB attenuator gives values of attenuation between each of the 10 dB steps. The audiometer hearing loss dial with its dB markings is nothing more than an attenuator calibrated in steps of 5 dB (or less).

A frequent application of the attenuator in audiology is to reduce the level of sound delivered to an earphone or loudspeaker, which is accomplished by reducing the level of the voltage to the loudspeaker or earphone. If the steps of the attenuator are linear (i.e., result in the same amount of reduction for each step), they may be easily calibrated by placing the attenuator in its

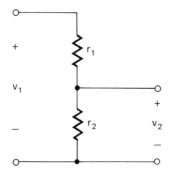

Figure 6.4 Circuit design of a voltage divider.

position of least attenuation and applying the system's maximum voltage to the loudspeaker or earphones. The output level of the sound at the minimum level of attenuation will then be known, and because the steps of attenuation are linear, the output at maximum attenuation will be known as well. This is exactly how the attenuators on an audiometer function and is precisely why we go to the trouble to calibrate the audiometer's sound output and attenuator linearity.

MIXERS

Sometimes the output signals from more than one source must be added together before being sent on to the remainder of the equipment. An example of this is in mixing a prerecorded sound source with that from a "live" microphone and having both of these signals presented from the same loudspeaker. You may think that this would be a simple matter of somehow combining the output wires of the equipment. When the equipment is combined, however, each piece of equipment "sees" the output impedance of the other; if they are the same, a short occurs and very little if any of the original signal is realized. To prevent this, devices called **mixers** are used in the sequence of instrumentation. A mixer has several channels of input and perhaps as few as one or two channels of output. Each input channel has a small amplifier associated with it so that the signal on that channel is boosted before being mixed. Sometimes these amplifiers are under the control of the operator, sometimes not. The mixer pictured in Figure 6.5 has individual "slider" type attenuators for each channel of input/output.

Because of special circuit characteristics, such as those shown in Figure 6.6, the output impedances of the individual amplifiers do not interfere with one another, and each of the channels of information is kept separate until the very last point in the circuit.

Mixers can also be used in reverse if you have an application that requires one signal to be split to several other channels. This application is useful, for example, if you want to make multiple simultaneous tape recordings of the same signal.

FILTERS

Filters, as the name implies, are devices for separating out certain portions of a complex waveform. A **filter** is a circuit that has a deliberately nonuniform transfer function with respect to frequency. The **transfer function** of any system is the ratio of its output waveform to its input waveform and is usually expressed in terms of both its magnitude as well as its phase shift. A filter can

Figure 6.5 Mixer. (Source: Photo courtesy of Radio Shack, a division of Tandy Corporation)

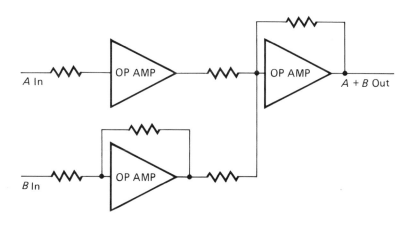

Figure 6.6 Circuit design of a typical mixer.

produce alterations in both the amplitude of frequency components of the input waveform as well as its phase relationships.

There are many types of filters, but one characteristic is common to all of them: Their gain or loss varies with the frequency of the signal that is input to them. Most filters are designed to "pass" certain frequencies and "reject" others. Filters generally come in four types: high pass, low pass, band pass, and band reject. In addition to this division, filters also come in analog form as well as digital form. Beyond this, filters may be active (i.e., amplify what they pass) or passive (i.e., have no amplifier).

1. **Low Pass Filters.** Low pass filters usually pass frequencies (offer minimal opposition to energy transfer) from their "cutoff" frequency down to DC, as illustrated in Figure 6.7a. It is important to remember that a low pass filter can also be referred to as a high cut filter as it "cuts" the higher frequencies.

2. **High Pass Filters.** High pass filters usually pass frequencies (offer minimal opposition to energy transfer) above some "cutoff" frequency, as illustrated in Figure 6.7b. A high pass filter can also be referred to as a low cut filter as it "cuts" the lower frequencies.

3. **Band Pass Filters.** Band pass filters pass signals that fall between two cutoff values. These filters can have differing bandwidths that may be adjustable or preset. If the pass band of the filter is relatively narrow, it is called a narrow band filter. If it is one octave wide, it is called a one-octave filter, and so on. Figure 6.8a shows a typical frequency response of a band pass filter.

4. **Band Reject Filter.** Band reject filters attenuate all frequencies that fall between two cutoff values. Typically, if these filters have a narrow band of rejection, they are termed "notch" filters because they notch out a section of the spectrum. Band reject filters are frequently used to isolate the line frequency (60 Hz) from the rest of the equipment to prevent 60 Hz "hum." A typical band reject filter response is shown in Figure 6.8b.

Analog and Digital Filters

Analog filters make use of the frequency characteristics of a collection of inductors and capacitors connected together in an electrical circuit. Inductance

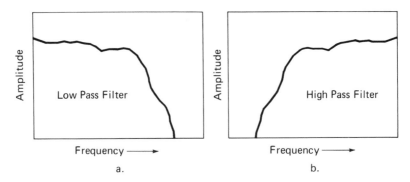

Figure 6.7 Frequency response of (a) a low pass filter and (b) a high pass filter.

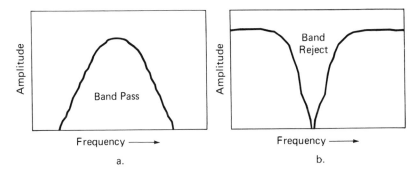

Figure 6.8 Frequency response of (a) a band pass filter and (b) a band reject filter.

is the electrical equivalent of mass and therefore works against the transfer of high-frequency information. Capacitance is the electrical equivalent of compliance, or stiffness, and therefore works against the transfer of low frequencies. (For a review of these concepts see Chapter 1).

Digital filters, as the name implies, work through a process of mathematics. With an understanding of the spectral content of the signal to be filtered, all frequencies of the signal can be reduced to numbers (analog-to-digital conversion), and then numbers that represent frequencies outside of the pass band and that are not wanted can be rejected. Figure 6.9 shows the analog signal going into the analog-to-digital (A/D) converter where it is converted to a series of numbers. The numerical signal is then transformed in the opposite direction (digital-to-analog), and the signal comes out minus the unwanted frequencies. The advantage of digital filters lies in their precision. Digital filters can be easily designed to exceed the capabilities of analog filters with their arrays of resistors, inductors, and capacitors.

Active and Passive Filters

Active filters are analog filters with circuits that contain amplifiers in addition to the resistance components (resistors) and the reactance components (capac-

Figure 6.9 Schematic of the process of digital filtering.

itors and inductors). These amplifiers allow the filters to increase the amplitude of the wanted signal over those of the unwanted portions of the signal. They are generally capable of very wide ranges of adjustment, have a wide dynamic range, have good linearity, and achieve much better performance than do passive filters. In addition, they will have controls for easy selection of band pass or band reject capability. If they are dual high/low band pass (two filters in one), their inputs and outputs may be interconnected to achieve twice the effect of either filter alone. These filters do require a power source so that they are not quite as portable as the passive filter.

Passive filters are analog filters that do their work on the basis of the natural ability of certain electrical components (resistors, capacitors, and inductors) to attenuate the signal. Because these filters have no external power and work by attenuating unwanted frequencies, they usually do not have the selectivity that an active filter might have. In addition, because there is no amplification, there is always some "insertion loss" — which means that the filter uses up some of the input energy, and amplification may need to be used on the output side to boost the signal. Unlike active filters, passive filters are difficult to design with easy switching capability between high pass and low pass. Consequently, the best one can hope for is a passive filter that has both a high pass side and a low pass side that can be joined for creating band pass capability.

Time Constants of Filters

It is important to keep in mind that as analog filter characteristics are changed, varying amounts of time delay are introduced between the input signal and the output signal. This is a natural function of the analog circuitry, and because of the electrical properties of the filter it will have a certain **time constant,** or reaction time. If the time constant of the filter is slower than the time constant of the input waveform, the filter will alter the shape of the waveform. Then such things as phase changes will occur. Figure 6.10 shows the output result on one type of signal when the filter characteristics are changed. The input waveform (sinusoid) is the top trace. The lower three traces result from changes to the filter's settings that produce increasingly narrow band passes. Notice the overall distortion of the signal's shape as well as the time delay introduced. Time constant problems are not a consideration when using digital filters.

Filter Rejection Rates

It is important to realize that if you adjust a filter to reject frequencies above or below a certain point this rejection is not infinite. Figure 6.11 shows an ideal filter pass band as well as what, in practice, the pass band usually looks like. There will be some amount of the signal left above or below the cutoff point.

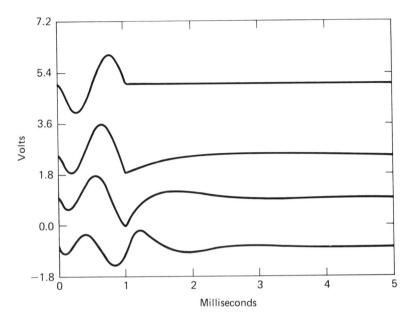

Figure 6.10 Effect of varying filter time constant on the resulting output waveform.

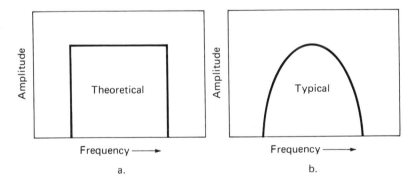

Figure 6.11 Frequency response of a filter having (a) an infinitely steep rejection rate and (b) a more typical rejection rate.

The amount of signal that is left is a function of the **roll-off rate** of the filter, or the rate of rejection. This roll-off rate is referred to as the filter "skirt." With an analog filter, it is impossible to achieve infinite filtering or a rectangular rejection rate, but it is possible with a digital filter under the right circumstances.

As a general statement, the steeper the skirt, the more selective will be the filter. The skirt rolls off at a rate specified by the internal construction of the filter. Passive filters rarely achieve roll-off rates of more than 18 dB per octave, whereas active filters and digital filters can achieve much higher rates of rejection — perhaps as much as 96 dB per octave.

Determining Roll-Off Rates and Cutoff Frequencies

The most widely used method for determining the cutoff frequency of a filter is to find the point on the filter skirt at which the signal energy or filter output is at 50% of peak value. Because we know that pressure is proportional to the square root of intensity, we can calculate where on the skirt this cutoff frequency lies. This frequency is equal to the point at which the sound pressure drops to 70.7% of full pressure (square root of 50%). This point is conveniently 3 dB below peak and is referred to as the "3 dB down point" or the half-power point.

In defining the characteristics of the filter, knowing the cutoff point is not enough. We also need to know the rate at which frequencies above and below the cutoff are rejected, or the roll-off rate. Normally, this rate is measured in terms of dB per octave. If, for example, we have a low pass filter that attenuates frequencies above the cutoff frequency at a rate of 6 dB per octave, this means that above the half-power point the sound power decreases by twofold for each doubling of frequency. Figure 6.12 illustrates these concepts. With the cutoff frequency specified and the roll-off rate specified, we can have a relatively clear image of what the filtered output spectrum of the input signal will look like.

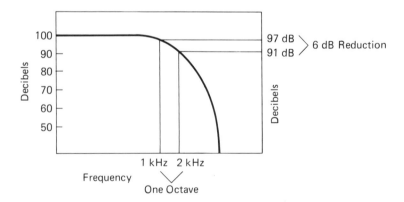

Figure 6.12   Pass band of a filter having a roll-off rate of 6 dB per octave.

Filter Resolution

Instead of simply rejecting all the information above or below some cutoff frequency, we may want to isolate discrete areas of the signal. This process would, of course, call for a filter such as a band pass filter, one that would segment units of a determined band width from the total signal. The decision that has to be made immediately is how fine or discrete do we wish the units of segmentation to be. In large part that depends on some prior knowledge of the frequency and amplitude complexity of the signal and the use we want to make of the filtered signal.

Always keep in mind that what is gotten from the filter in terms of output depends on the method that you have chosen to display the results, as well as the size of the filter's pass band. In many ways the simplest method to determine signal intensities within filter output bandwidths is simply to measure the decibel value of the filter's output with a sound level meter. The problem with doing this is that the sound level meter integrates (i.e., sums) all the energy in the output bandwidth and gives only a single decibel value for all the energy in the filter's bandwidth. As a result, this single decibel value has to stand for all the individual frequency activity encompassed within the filter's band pass. In other words, energy is summed across the entire band pass, and individual deviations from that summed, or mean, value cannot be observed. If we adopt this approach and we are faced with a very complex signal with a good deal of amplitude fluctuations, such as speech, then the size of the band pass of the filter becomes a critical issue. If the pass band chosen is too wide, the signal will not be well resolved, and the amplitude value of the pass band will not be really representative of the signal's configuration.

In Figure 6.13 we have measured the same waveform with two kinds of band pass filters — the one on the left having an adjustable one-octave band pass and that on the right having an adjustable one-third-octave band pass. We can see that the measured decibel value outputs (open dots) of each of the one-third-octave filters is much more representative of the amplitude envelope of the signal than those of the one-octave filters. The more narrow the pass band of the filter becomes, the more the filter band outputs resemble the actual signal and the more completely the complex signal will have been analyzed.

LABORATORY EXERCISE

In this exercise you will interconnect several pieces of equipment and use them to listen to filtered speech. You can refer to the equipment flowchart in Figure 6.14 for help with the exercise. This exercise requires the use of the following equipment:

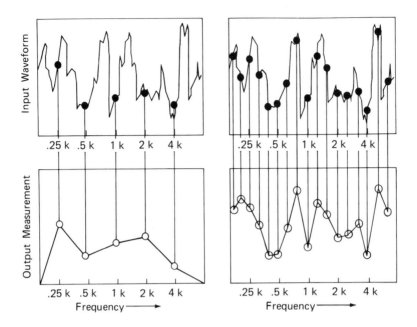

Figure 6.13 (top) Input waveform, (bottom) output waveforms filtered through (left) one octave and (right) one third octave filters.

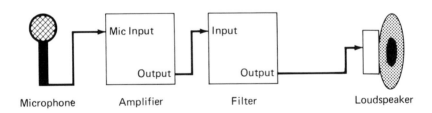

Figure 6.14 Equipment flowchart for the laboratory exercise.

- Microphone (any type will do).
- Amplifier (must have volume control and microphone input).
- Filter (any type will do).
- Loudspeaker or headphones.

Step 1.   Carefully connect each of the pieces of equipment. The microphone goes into the "mic" input of the amplifier. The output of the amplifier is connected to the input of the filter. The output of the filter is connected to the headphones or the loudspeaker. All the input/output connectors are likely to be different, so this exercise will give you a chance to practice what you learned in Chapter 2.

Step 2.   Speak into the microphone while you adjust the filter so that you can hear a difference in the quality of your voice. It will make no difference if you use a high, low, or band pass on the filter so long as you can hear a difference in the way your voice sounds as you adjust the filter.

Step 3.   Experiment with various filter settings. First, filter out the low frequencies in your voice (high pass filtering), and listen as the vowel sounds disappear. Next, filter out the high frequencies (low pass filtering), and listen to your voice without consonant sounds. Note: Because you will hear your voice through the bones of your skull (bone conduction), you will have to keep the volume level high to mask this effect. After you have read other chapters of this book, you may wish to try this exercise again using a tape recording of your voice and comparing the difference.

KEY TERMS

active filter	low pass filter
analog filter	mixer
amplifier	operational amplifier
attenuator	passive filter
band pass filter	preamplifier
band reject filter	roll-off rate step
differential amplification	attenuator
digital filter	time constant
filter	transfer function
gain	transfer function
high pass filter	voltage divider

SUGGESTED READINGS

Carr, Joseph J., *The Complete Handbook of Amplifiers, Oscillators, and Multivibrators* (1st ed.). Blue Ridge Summit, PA: Tab Books, 1981.

Curtis, Jack F., and Martin C. Schultz. *Basic Laboratory Instrumentation for Speech and Hearing.* Boston: Little, Brown, 1986.

Rockland Systems Corp. "The Application of Filters to Analog and Digital Signal Processing," West Nyack, NY: Rockland Systems Corp., 1977.

Strong, Peter. *Biophysical Measurement.* Beaverton, OR: Tektronix, Inc., 1970.

CHAPTER 7

CRT Displays, Oscilloscopes, Recorders, and Plotters

Most of the signals measured by a speech pathologist or audiologist are acoustic signals. Sometimes they are motion signals – for example, lip movement or rib cage expansion. You must always keep in mind that these kinds of signals cannot be measured directly. In the case of sound, we cannot see the change of the energy in the air. In the case of lip movement, we cannot see the tiny changes in position that occur. There must be some way of displaying these signals in a form that can be adequately measured. For this reason, all signals are converted by transducers (see Chapter 3) into an electrical analog of the original waveform. This electrical energy is then sent to a recording device that allows for the temporary or permanent display of the data. The original signal can then be measured along some parameter, compared with some other signal, or stored for later use.

The type of display device selected is often dictated by cost, but the type of signal being recorded usually also has some bearing on the decision. For example, if a signal is to be recorded over a long period (several minutes or hours), the choice would probably be a chart recorder because this device permits the display of data on a strip of paper that comes out of the recorder in a continuous role. If the signal is of brief duration and there is no particular need to save the display, an oscilloscope with its fast-reacting light beam may be the choice. What these devices have in common is that they alter the electrical representation of the data to a form that is easily appreciated by the eye.

In this chapter, we explore the characteristics of the major pieces of recording equipment likely to be used in the clinic or laboratory. Included in this discussion is a description of the major controls on these devices, how they may be used to record speech and hearing data, and the advantages and disadvantages of one device over another.

CRT DISPLAYS

One of the most common and most versatile methods of displaying data is the **cathode ray tube (CRT)** display. These displays are the basis for TV, oscilloscope, computer, and other kinds of displays. Because CRTs are all around us and are used frequently by us, it is important for us to have some knowledge of how they function. A CRT display consists of the following components:

- A large vacuum tube, the front end of which has a coating of phosphorus.
- A source of electrons.
- A mechanism for shaping the source of electrons into a tight beam and for bending the beam left or right and up or down.

Figure 7.1 shows these components as they might appear in a standard CRT. The electrons are produced by heating a filament of metal called the **cathode**, which throws off electrons into the vacuum inside the tube. These negatively charged particles are attracted across the space of the vacuum tube and through a focusing section by an opposite (positive) charge called the **anode**. As these particles travel across from the cathode to the anode, they pass through a strong and controllable magnetic field. The magnetic field is produced by the influence of two sets of deflectors. The vertical deflectors are controlled by the amplitude fluctuations of the signal, and the horizontal deflectors are controlled by a time-base generator (clock). The electron beam is then deflected in the vertical direction according to the amplitude fluctuations of the electrical current that represents, for example, the speech waveform, and in the horizontal direction by the time necessary to view or complete the waveform. The moving beam of electrons then falls on the phosphor screen and causes the phosphor to glow, and we see a moving spot of light.

The principal advantage of the CRT display is that the light beam, unlike a moving needle or writing pen, has virtually no mass to interfere with the faithful reproduction of the waveform. All other instruments that depend for recording on the movement of a pen or some other type of meter needle

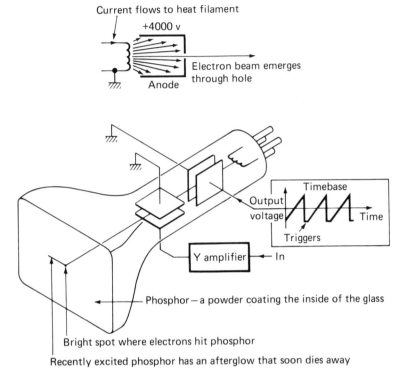

Figure 7.1 Schematic of a typical CRT display device. (Source: *Electronics in the Life Sciences,* Steven Young. London: Macmillan Press, 1973. Reprinted with permission.)

introduce some averaging of the rapid transitions of the signal because of the mass of the system. This averaging process is referred to as the **damping constant** of the recording system. The greater the damping constant, the less likely the system is to reproduce rapidly changing waveforms with fidelity.

OSCILLOSCOPES

An **oscilloscope** is an instrument that is capable of displaying an electrical signal on a CRT. An oscilloscope is differentiated from a simple CRT by the various controls used to control the CRT display. The oscilloscope can be an important instrument for the speech pathologist or the audiologist because it can be used for a variety of measurement problems. Oscilloscopes are available that are small and easy to carry so that they may be used in the clinic to display speech signals to patients in therapy, carried to classrooms for demonstrations to students, and used in the laboratory for calibration purposes. A picture of a typical oscilloscope is shown in Figure 7.2.

Components and Controls

Most oscilloscopes consist of three general divisions of components. First, as we have discussed, they have a CRT display, which usually has a grid superimposed on the glass that may be four or five divisions high and 10 divisions wide. This grid is used in conjunction with the calibrated vertical and horizontal amplifier sections of the oscilloscope to give a reference for amplitude of the signal and total time across the face of the CRT. Most of the settings for amplitude and time on the oscilloscope are given in terms of amplitude per division or time per division. Refer again to Figure 7.2, where it can be seen that the display of the oscilloscope shows a sinusoidal waveform having an amplitude of four divisions. Because the vertical amplifier has been set to 0.5 v per division, the peak-to-peak voltage of the sinusoid is 2 v.

Time Base Controls.   The time base section of the oscilloscope works when you apply a controlled and changing voltage to the horizontal deflection plates

Figure 7.2   Typical oscilloscope with a 2-v peak-peak sinusoid display.

of the CRT. In this manner, the change of voltage is made to occur either faster or slower, depending on the settings that you choose. The time base is calibrated in terms of time per distance (or per division on the screen), and the signal is displayed over distance (several divisions). For example, if you choose a time setting that causes the beam (light) to travel across the screen at the rate of one division every second and there are 10 divisions across the screen, then the total signal time that you can display will be 10 sec.

Vertical Amplifier Controls. To display the amplitude changes of the signal, the oscilloscope has a vertical amplifier. The settings on the amplifier determine the amplification of the signal being displayed; such amplitude is calibrated as voltage per distance (or per division on the screen). For example, if the signal being displayed is the speech waveform and the peak-to-peak display equals five divisions with an amplifier setting of 1 v per division, peak-to-peak voltage of the signal is 5 v.

External Trigger. In addition to the two previously mentioned basic sections and controls, many oscilloscopes have features that allow for certain other aspects of signal control and measurement. For example, it may be necessary to capture a very fast-moving signal such as the onset of a pure tone or the production of a consonant. In such a case, initiate (i.e., trigger) the sweep of the oscilloscope beam at the start of the signal. To enable you to do this, an external trigger arrangement is included that automatically instigates the sweep at the moment you apply the signal to the vertical amplifier. By this means, you can trigger the oscilloscope before, during, or after the onset of the signal. In most applications, the triggering of the scope is done at the onset of the signal. You can most easily accomplish this by simply splitting the signal to the external trigger input as well as to the vertical amplifier input. The alternative is either to trigger the scope's sweep manually just at the instant of the signal onset or to place the scope in a repetitive sweep mode and try to produce the signal when the beam is traveling across the screen. Neither of these schemes works well if the signal is a rapid one.

Multiple Channel Waveform Storage. Two other features that are found on some scopes and that can be useful are (1) multiple channel capability, and (2) the ability to save, or store, the display called waveform storage. Multiple channel capability simply means that the scope has two separate vertical amplifiers and may in addition have two or more independently controllable time bases. This allows for the display of several different signals at the same time on either the same or a different sweep speed. For example, you may wish to display on channel one the electrical waveform that is being fed into an earphone and at the same time display the acoustic waveform coming from the earphone on channel two. It would then be easy to compare the characteristics of the transducer on the input waveform. When the waveform is not repetitive and is brief, close inspection of it is difficult if not impossible. However, with a storage scope, you can "freeze" the waveform display on the screen for an indefinite period for long-term inspection.

There are many other features and controls on the typical oscilloscope, but they are beyond the basic discussion of this text. In selecting a scope to use for a given task, give some initial thought to the requirements of the measurements to be made. The wise choice is then to select the scope that meets these minimum requirements. Thereby, you avoid having to use a scope with a confusing array of controls and options that are superfluous to your needs. You should always review the owner's manual that comes with the scope. By inputting a known signal, such as a sinusoid from a **function generator** and using the manual as a guide, with some experimentation you can learn on your own what the various controls can do. Some examples of oscilloscope operation are in the laboratory exercises at the end of this chapter.

RECORDERS AND PLOTTERS

Although the oscilloscope is a versatile instrument, frequently the display of data calls for a more permanent record. If you wish to display data so that it can be stored and then recalled for additional measurement you should use a graphic level recorder or a plotter. Plotters are output devices that plot changing amplitude against time with a moving pen on a stationary strip of paper. Plotters are used to measure short-term signal events. Recorders measure long-term signal events on a movable strip of paper. The two most frequently used types of recorders and plotters are the strip chart recorder and the X–Y plotter.

The functions of these pieces of hardware are increasingly being taken over by computers. Data can be recorded by a computer, stored on floppy disks, and then brought up for additional review when desired. However, there are still limitations to this type of measurement scheme, not the least of which is expense and a lack of versatility if you have limited ability with the computer.

Strip Chart Recorders

The **strip chart recorder** (see Figure 7.3) operates on the principle of a pen moving across a strip of moving paper. The major limitation of this system is that the mechanical components of the system contribute to the overall mass and inertia problems that have been discussed elsewhere. This problem usually limits the upper frequency response of the strip chart recorder to about 100 Hz. Practically, this means that signals with periodicity's greater than 100 Hz or signals that change direction abruptly cannot be accurately recorded by a

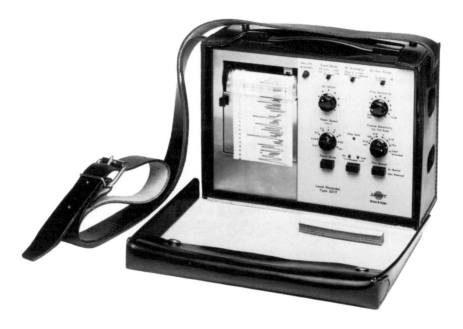

Figure 7.3 Typical strip chart recorder. (Source: Courtesy Bruel & Kjaer Instruments, Inc., Marlborough, MA)

strip chart system. Nevertheless, for the collection and permanent display of certain slow-moving signals over long periods, the strip chart recorder can be a valuable asset in the clinic or lab.

The basic operative principle of the strip recorder is that the signal applied to the recorder causes the voltage to change in the pen system. This causes the pen to rise and fall across the strip of paper and to represent the signal as a pattern of inked lines. Usually the paper has lines or a grid printed on it so that the pen's movements can be calibrated to this grid. In addition, the recorder has a control that allows the sensitivity of the pen to be increased or decreased by some amount to accommodate signals of differing amplitude.

While the pen is moving across the paper, the paper is also moving, usually coming off a large roll. The speed with which the paper moves under the pen ultimately determines the time base across which the lines are drawn. Paper speed is also controllable and in conjunction with the grid marks on the paper allows for precise measurement of passing time. Calibration of this type of system is easily accomplished by applying a sinusoid of known frequency and amplitude to the input of the system and then adjusting the pen sensitivity controls until a suitable deflection of the pen is achieved. Calibration of time is accomplished with the paper speed controls and the knowledge of the period value of the input signal.

X-Y Plotters

The X-Y plotter (see Figure 7.4) usually differs from the strip chart recorder in that the paper remains stationary in a holder. The pen is then caused to move in both the X (horizontal) and the Y (vertical) directions across the paper. The paper is printed with grid marks to facilitate the eventual measurement of the signal. The movement of the pen can be calibrated for both the amplitude (Y axis) of the signal and the time of display (X axis) for the signal. The X-Y plotter is not as useful for signals of long duration as are strip chart recorders, although they can be used for such purposes. Usually, if you try to put a long-duration signal on $8\frac{1}{2}$ by 11 inch X-Y plotter paper, the signal is so condensed that individual components of it may not be visible. For this reason, X-Y plotters are most useful for signals of short duration such as evoked auditory responses, the activity on a tympanometer, or brief speech utterances.

LABORATORY EXERCISES

Exercise One

This exercise requires the use of a microphone and an oscilloscope. The purpose of the exercise is to familiarize you with the basic controls on the

Figure 7.4 Typical X-Y plotter.

oscilloscope. The best way to do this is to follow along in the operator's manual for the scope while progressing through each of the steps that follow. Once you have mastered the basic controls, you should continue to experiment with the other controls. See Figure 7.5 for help with the exercise.

Step 1. Connect the microphone to the oscilloscope's input. If the scope has an external trigger capability take care not to plug the microphone into the trigger input. Sometimes they look the same, but their function is not the same.

Step 2. Place the scope in the free run mode. Consult the manual for the proper control to turn.

Step 3. Adjust the time base control so that the sweep of the light beam takes approximately 10 msec per division.

Step 4. Speak into the microphone when the light beam first appears at the left side of the display. Use a sustained vowel such as [i] or [a].

Step 5. By using the divisions on the face of the display, try to estimate the time between each of the major peaks in the waveform. These peaks should have a fairly periodic appearance. By substituting this time estimation into the formula $f = 1/t$ where t equals your time estimate in milliseconds, and f equals frequency, you will be able to calculate the lowest frequency (fundamental) in your voice.

Step 6. Change the time base (sweep time) so that the light beam travels across the display at the rate of about 1 sec per division.

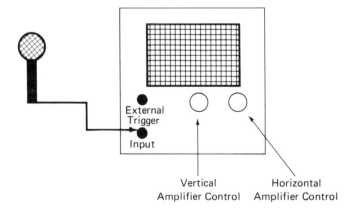

Figure 7.5 Exercise One equipment flowchart.

Step 7.   Speak a phrase into the microphone and observe the amplitude fluctuations that accompany the speech signal.

Exercise Two

In this exercise you will learn to use the oscilloscope's external triggering capability to capture a brief event. For this exercise you need a storage oscilloscope. This type of scope can be identified by looking for the words "store" or "storage" on the control panel of the scope. If you cannot decide if your scope is a storage scope, you will either have to study the operations manual or ask your instructor for help.

Step 1.   You will need to attach the microphone to both the input of the oscilloscope as well as to the connector marked "external trigger." Because your scope will most probably have BNC connectors, the easiest way to accomplish this connection is to attach a BNC "T" connector to either the signal input or the trigger input. In this manner, the input signal can be split to both inputs.

Step 2.   Place the scope in the external triggered position. Consult the operations manual for help in identifying the proper control(s) to turn.

Step 3.   Adjust the time base so that the entire display will take about 50 msec. This will mean adjusting to about 5 msec per division and will produce a display that is so brief that without the aid of external triggering you would be unable to see much detail in the sweep.

Step 4.   Using the sound [pa] or [ta], speak into the microphone and adjust the sensitivity of the external trigger so that the sweep starts at the instant that you release the plosive part of the sound.

Step 5.   If you have been able to accomplish the storage of either the [pa] or the [ta], you will be able to see a detailed display of the amplitude pulses associated with your voice. If you are a male, you may see as many as four to five of these, and if you are a female as many as 10. In addition, in the front portion of the display you may be able to see the space between the onset of the [p] or [t] and the onset of vocalization. This is known as voice onset time (VOT).

Step 6.   Now reduce the sweep time to about 10 to 20 msec per division and repeat the process. Now you should be able to examine the VOT a little bit better. Try experimenting with the difference between [ta] and [da] or [pa] and [ba]. Is the VOT different for these pairs?

Exercise Three

In this experiment you will again use the external triggering capability, this time to look at the rise time of an audiometric stimulus. In doing this experiment, you will use both channels of the scope so that you can look at the electrical waveform to the earphone and the acoustic waveform from the earphone at the same time. You will need a scope with two-channel capability as well as external triggering. In addition you will need an audiometer (any portable one will do), and you will need a sound level meter (SLM) with an output marked AC. If such an SLM is not available, you can accomplish this experiment with a microphone in place of the SLM. See Figure 7.6 for additional help.

Step 1. Remove the earphone cord from one of the output channels of the audiometer. Insert into that output connector a "Y" patch cord adapter that has phone plug receptacles on either branch of the "Y."

Step 2. Insert the earphone cord into one side of the "Y" adapter and another patch cord into the other side. Route the extra patch cord to the external trigger input of the oscilloscope, and with a "T" connector split that signal to the signal input of the right channel of the scope.

Step 3. If you are using an SLM, put the earphone over the standard 6 cc coupler and connect the coupler to the SLM. Insert a patch cord into the AC

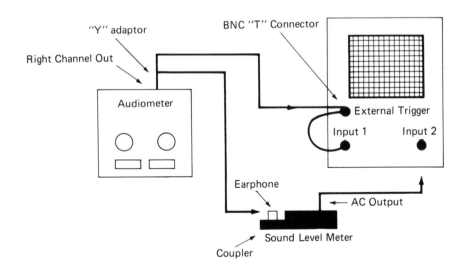

Figure 7.6 Exercise Three equipment flowchart.

output of the SLM and route it to the signal input of the left channel of the scope. Turn on the SLM and adjust its sensitivity to get a mid-meter deflection when you activate the audiometer. If you are using a microphone instead of the SLM, then you can lay the earphone down next to the microphone and run the microphone cord to the left channel of the scope.

Step 4.   In this step you must adjust the sensitivity of the scope's external trigger. First, adjust the time base controls for both channels so that you have a full screen display of about 200 msec or 20 msec per division. You may have to make this shorter or longer as you make the remainder of the trigger adjustments. Next you must repeatedly depress the audiometer's interrupter switch to activate the signal while you adjust the trigger so that the scope triggers at the moment you introduce the sound. Note: It is important to get as much sensitivity as possible here so that you will be able to see the leading edge of the signal as the voltage rises. Do not be concerned with the trailing edge; in fact, you may not even be able to see it because the sweep time will be too fast.

Step 5.   If all is working as detailed, you should be able to see the electrical signal to the earphone on the right channel and the acoustic signal from the phone on the left channel. Now, by using the calibration of the horizontal time base control, you will be able to calculate the rise time of the audiometer. It ought to be about 25 msec if the audiometer is in calibration.

KEY TERMS

anode	function generator
cathode	oscilloscope
cathode ray tube (CRT)	strip chart recorder
damping constant	X–Y plotter

SUGGESTED READINGS

Curtis, Jack F., and Martin C. Schultz. *Basic Laboratory Instrumentation for Speech and Hearing.* Boston: Little, Brown, 1986.

Lenk, John D. *Handbook of Oscilloscopes: Theory and Application.* Englewood Cliffs, NJ: Prentice-Hall, 1982.

McPherson, David L., and John W. Thatcher. *Instrumentation in the Hearing Sciences.* New York: Grune & Stratton, 1977.

Young, Stephen. *Electronics in the Life Sciences.* New York: Halsted Press, 1973.

CHAPTER 8

Analog and Digital Magnetic Tape Recorders

Perhaps no other piece of instrumentation is as universally used in the speech and hearing clinic or laboratory as the tape recorder. In fact, if you take a casual stroll through the average clinic you will usually sight a dozen or more tape recorders. We take for granted the use of tape recorders for storing the sound of the human voice. We may not be so familiar with the techniques of making good recordings or with understanding the way in which the recording process actually works, however. The purpose of this chapter is to explore the recorder and the recording process in some detail so that you can put this piece of instrumentation to work to its fullest potential.

ADVANTAGES OF TAPE RECORDING

In terms of instrumentation, tape recorders offer many advantages: Tape recorders have a wide frequency response; there is a minimal amount of processing involved; the recording can be monitored as soon as it is made; tape can be stored for long periods of time; multichannel information can be recorded; and tape recorders allow the user to adjust the time. In the following paragraphs we will briefly discuss these advantages.

Wide Frequency Response.   As will be seen in sections to come, frequency response is dependent on several factors in the recording process, such as head gap dimension and tape transport speed. Using tape speeds as high as 120 ips (inches per second) can result in recording frequencies as high or higher than 50 MHz. Using frequency modulation (FM) recording techniques can result in the recording of information with frequencies as low as direct current (DC).

Minimal Processing.   Unlike film there is no lengthy delay in processing the final results of tape recording. Tape may be replayed as soon as it is rewound.

Instantaneous Monitoring of Recording.   If the tape recorder has the playback head situated just after the record head, the actual recording can be heard within less than a second. Because of this, fine adjustment of the recording parameters can be made during the process.

Storage.   With the proper cautions, tape can be stored indefinitely without loss of the signal. In addition, the tape may be recorded and erased and rerecorded many times without loss of fidelity.

Multichannel Information.   Tape recorders with multiple channel recording capability are easy to use for recording several different but simultaneous events. Quarter-inch tape can typically carry as many as eight independent tracks of recorded information.

Adjustable Time Base.   Time can be manipulated easily by changing recording and playback speed. Recordings can be made at very high speeds to capture complex events and then played back at very slow speeds to allow for ease of analysis. The reverse is equally true, and in some cases valuable analysis time can be saved by analyzing at two or three times the original speed of the recording.

KINDS OF TAPE RECORDERS

Both analog and digital tape recorders are available today. Digital recorders and digital audio tape (DAT) are relatively recent developments and have an associated high cost attendant to them. Nevertheless, DAT may be available to you in your clinic or laboratory, so we shall have some things to say about them in this chapter. The primary discussion, however, will focus on analog recorders and analog recording tape as these are the items that most undergraduates will encounter.

ANALOG TAPE RECORDERS

Analog tape recorders generally come in two broad categories: direct and frequency modulation (FM). In a **direct recording**, the sound is transferred to the tape directly with no intervening transduction stage. **Frequency modulation** tape recorders record the sound after first altering the frequency of the original signal through the process of frequency modulation. FM recorders are usually quite expensive and are used to record information that has slowly changing amplitude fluctuations. For example, recording the rise and fall of the chest during respiration has a periodicity much too slow to be recorded in a direct fashion. The frequency of the respiratory cycle is much lower than the lower limit of the frequency response of the direct recorder. With an FM recorder or with an FM recording adapter sequenced with a direct recorder, you can easily record the movement of the chest during respiration.

Most direct tape recorders today are of the stereo variety—that is, they have the ability to record two or more separate tracks of information on the same tape. Anyone thinking of purchasing a tape recorder for standard clinic or lab work ought to have at least two-channel capability. This capability would, for example, allow the clinician to record comments on one track while recording the client's speech on the other track. Another useful advantage to having two tracks is that a target utterance can be recorded in repetitive fashion on one track, and the client's attempts to approximate the target can be recorded on the opposite track. Later the client can listen to both and gain some appreciation of improvement. Figure 8.1 shows the various types of record and playback heads and tape track arrangements.

Tape recorders are also differentiated on the basis of whether they work with open reels of tape (open reel recorders) or tape that is prepackaged in a cassette (cassette recorders). In the past it was thought that the cassette recorder was not capable of the same fidelity as the open reel recorder, but that distinction is of less concern today and, in fact, an open reel recorder may be difficult to find in your clinic or laboratory.

Keep in mind that tape recorders are not solely for the storage of acoustic information. Virtually any type of activity that can be transduced into an electrical event can be stored on magnetic tape. Examples of such activity are the following:

Speech	Evoked potentials from the nervous system
Music	Eye movements
Telemetry data	Tongue, lip, and jaw movements
Computer data	Pressure changes
TV pictures and sound	Temperature changes
Respiration activity	

Many more kinds of information could be listed here, but the present list should suffice to let you see the wide range of storage possibilities afforded by magnetic tape.

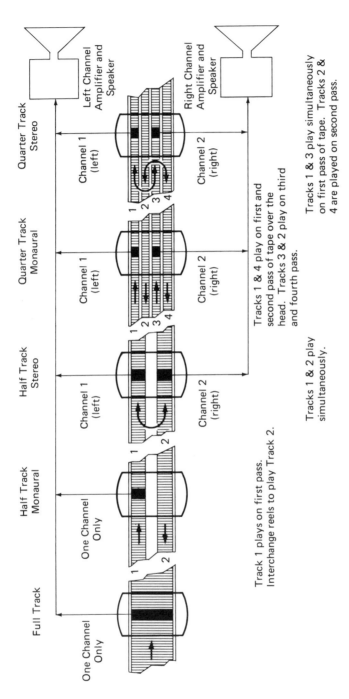

Figure 8.1 Tape head and track patterns. (Source: Viking 433 operations manual. Viking Tape Recorders, Minneapolis, MN. Reprinted with permission.)

THE RECORDING PROCESS

At the heart of the recording process is a magnetic field that is induced by changing voltages and created by the recording head of the recorder. Figure 8.2 shows a simple example of the construction of a record head. It consists of a metallic core surrounded by wire windings. The core is separated by an air gap across which the tape is transported. The signal to be recorded is transduced (by the transducer) to electrical current, and that current is applied to the windings of the core. The alterations in the strength of the current create a varying electromagnetic field across the air gap. The variations in the magnetic field are then transferred in a proportional manner to the metal material that is on the tape—thus permanently magnetizing the tape. On playback of the recorded material, the magnetized tape moves across the air gap of the playback head. The fluctuating magnetic field on the tape causes fluctuations in the magnetic field of the core and induces current to flow in the windings of the playback head. The current changes are then amplified and further processed by the remainder of the circuitry of the tape recorder.

In addition to the record head and the playback head, the recorder has an erase head. The erase head usually precedes the record head so that the tape is continually erased just before it crosses the record head. This can sometimes be a disadvantage if you wish to record material over that which has already been recorded without erasing the original recording (sound-on-sound recording). To accomplish sound-on-sound recording, you must buy a tape recorder with

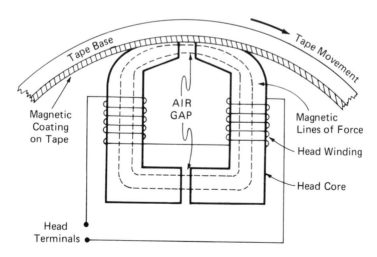

Figure 8.2 Construction details of the record head of a tape recorder. (Source: *Instrumentation in the Hearing Sciences,* David L. McPherson. New York: Grune & Stratton, 1977, p. 152. Reprinted with permission.)

an erase head that can be turned off or else temporarily disabled. The process by which the tape is erased is simply to apply a very high frequency sinusoidal signal to the tape such that all previously recorded material is replaced by the high frequency. The frequency chosen is beyond the capabilities of the remainder of the tape recorders circuitry to reproduce; consequently, it is never heard. The usual values for these erase signals are in the range of 50 to 75 kHz.

The range of frequencies that can be recorded depends on the size of the air gap on the record and reproduce heads and the speed with which the tape is transported across the heads. As the frequency response demands go up, the air gap must be made smaller or the tape speed must be made faster. Because the air gaps are usually constant, the only factor that can be manipulated is the tape speed. In general, if the tape recorder has multiple speed capability, the fastest speed should be used for such signals as music whereas a slower speed is satisfactory for such things as speech. You will recall that as the frequency of the activity being recorded goes down, the changing lines of force in the coil that are responsible for the magnetizing of the tape become slower until a point is reached at which the tape will no longer be magnetized. At this point, the information can no longer be recorded directly and an FM recorder is needed.

In the direct tape recorder, the signal is recorded directly onto the tape as voltage and frequency variations. In the FM tape recorder, voltage variations are also being recorded, but frequency information is recorded indirectly by frequency modulation. The FM recorder has what is called a **carrier frequency** that is usually high or at least near the center of the pass band of the recorder's frequency response. Let us say that the frequency is 10,000 Hz. Incoming frequency fluctuations from the original signal cause the carrier frequency to be increased or decreased by amounts equal to the original signal fluctuations. Consequently, what is recorded on the tape by the heads is not direct frequency information but, rather, frequency modulated (FM) information. Later in the process the remainder of the playback circuitry decodes these frequency modulations and reproduces them as replicas of the original frequency fluctuations.

Aside from the record, reproduce, and erase heads that already have been discussed, the tape recorder consists of other parts and circuitry of which you should have some knowledge, and they are discussed in the next section.

TAPE TRANSPORT AND RECORDING CONTROLS

The principle components of a tape recorder are its tape transport and recording controls.

The major function of the tape transport is to move the tape across the heads with a constant speed. If the speed is not constant, the result will be heard as a fluctuation in the pitch of the output known as **wow** (variations under 10 Hz) and **flutter** (variations greater than 10 Hz). Wow and flutter are not serious problems for simple voice recordings that will not be carefully measured. However, if the recordings are to be analyzed in such a manner that frequency, time, amplitude, and the like are important parameters, then tape transport speed must be kept constant. You can check transport speed by recording a pure tone at one speed and then playing back at the same speed as well as at any other speeds that may be available on the recorder. If, for example, the frequency was 500 Hz and was recorded at $3\frac{3}{4}$ ips, when the tape is played back at that speed the frequency should be the same. If played back at twice the tape speed (7 ips), it should be 1,000 Hz. At half the speed ($1\frac{7}{8}$ ips), it should be at 250 Hz. If this procedure results in variations that are beyond the manufacturer's specifications, return the recorder for recalibration of its tape speeds.

The tape transport mechanism must be able to move the tape backward and forward at fast speeds when you are searching for information, and it must be able to stop the tape very fast without tearing or stretching it. In general, most tape recorders have controls for activating "fast forward," "rewind," "forward or play," and "record." Normally, to record you must activate more than one control at the same time, usually "forward" and "record." This is a safety feature that prevents accidental recording or erasing of material.

Selection of speed of tape movement may not be an option on a cassette recorder but is on the open reel recorder. Standard tape speeds are $7\frac{1}{2}$, $3\frac{3}{4}$, and $1\frac{1}{8}$ ips. Selection of tape speed is determined by the type of recording you plan to make and the length of the tape on which you will record. For example, a standard open reel with 1,200 feet of tape will record for 30 min at $7\frac{1}{2}$ ips, 60 min at $3\frac{3}{4}$ ips, and 120 min at $1\frac{7}{8}$ ips. A slow speed such as $1\frac{7}{8}$ ips is certainly all right for recordings of voice that will be listened to only casually and not measured. However, if you intend to listen for such things as phonetic distortions or if you need to measure certain parameters of consonant production, then you should always use a faster tape speed. As a general rule, the faster the tape speed the better the fidelity of the recording.

In addition to tape transport controls, the standard recorder has, at a minimum, controls for adjusting the recording level (gain control), adjustment of the frequency emphasis of the recording (tone control), and some sort of a meter (volume unit meter) for monitoring the level of the recording as it is happening. The recorder may have other controls, but you should use the operator's manual for a particular recorder for additional explanation of those controls.

MAGNETIC TAPE

Most tapes are made from the same basic types of materials. The major differences among them seems to be the varying degrees of perfection attained in their construction, the frequency response obtainable, and the level of tape noise or **tape hiss**. The basic parts of magnetic tape are the nonmagnetic base, the magnetic powder, and the binder.

The primary requirement of the base is that it be thin, strong, flexible, and have a minimum of longitudinal stretch. There are basically two types of base materials in use today: polyester film and tensilized polyester (Mylar). Polyester film is the less expensive of the two, but it also has less dimensional stability and is more subject to tearing and breaking than the tensilized variety. Mylar is the tape base of choice for quality recordings and instrumentation-grade recorders. Tensilized tape has been prestretched and is much less likely to tear or break. The major problem with Mylar tape is that if something goes wrong in the recording process and the tape gets hung up, it will stretch a good deal before it breaks. This usually renders the tape useless, although sometimes low heat, like that from a hair dryer, will cause a bad stretch to return to its original dimension.

The backing material is cut into widths of $\frac{1}{4}$ in. (standard for audio tape recording) or $\frac{1}{2}$ to $\frac{3}{4}$ in. (for FM tape and video recording). When laminated with the magnetic material and the binder, the thickness is most commonly $\frac{1}{2}$, 1, or $1\frac{1}{2}$ mils. This thickness aspect leads to a trading relationship between flexibility and strength. The $\frac{1}{2}$-mil tape is the most flexible and gives the longest recording time per tape transport speed, although it is the weakest and most susceptible to stretch and other undesirable recording qualities. The $1\frac{1}{2}$ mil thickness gives the most strength, the least flexibility, and the shortest recording time.

The magnetic material can be any ferromagnetic material, but it usually consists of chromium dioxide, which has a uniform magnetization characteristic and uniform particle size. The material is spread on the base so that density and area are uniform. This uniform dispersion ensures the best signal-to-noise (S/N) ratios and the greatest effects related to the flux of the magnetic field in the record head. To achieve the greatest possible S/N ratios and to handle the widest possible range of frequencies, two layers of magnetic material may be spread on the tape. The layer that is closest to the tape heads is spread in a perpendicular direction to the longitudinal axis of the tape, and the particles in the layer farthest from the head are spread parallel to the longitudinal axis of the tape.

The binder material of the tape serves several purposes. It is an adhesive that binds the magnetic powder to the base, maintains the orientation and dispersion of the particles, and in many cases acts as a lubricant for the passage of the tape across the heads.

Tape-Caused Distortion

The great majority of distortion effects and the response characteristics of magnetic tape recordings are manifestations of the interactions of the entire tape system. Seldom is the total distortion effect the result of just one part of the system. Some of the distortions that can be caused by the tape itself are noise, print-through, and frequency distortion. Noise may be caused by any one or several of the following properties of the tape:

- Variations in particle size.
- Variations in the particle dispersion thickness.
- Stiffness of the tape.
- Abrasiveness of the tape coating.

The two major types of noise associated with the tape are **modulation** (characterized by fuzzy reproduction during the presence of the signal) and **drop-out** (characterized by the nonexistence of the signal). Drop-out is particularly a problem when recording steady-state signals and can be heard best when recording white noise. It is caused by discontinuities in the thickness of the coatings on the tape.

Print-through can occur in two ways. The first is called *fore-print* and is characterized by the sound of an echo preceding the signal. The second is called *after-print* and occurs when the echo follows the signal. In either case, the problem is caused by the interaction of the magnetic fields on the tape. When the tape is wound on the reel, one layer of it (the top layer in fore-print) causes an alteration in the layer just below it. Print-through is influenced by the following:

- Thickness of the tape.
- Temperature of the tape storage area.
- Amplitude of the original recording.

Manufacturers of magnetic tape usually publish a listing of their tapes that includes technical specifications. These spec sheets are useful to have when deciding what kind of tape to purchase for a particular recording job. An example of this information is shown in Figure 8.3.

DIGITAL TAPE RECORDERS AND DIGITAL AUDIO TAPE

This area of sound recording and reproduction is changing very rapidly and it is likely that what we write here will not be very representative in even 1 year's time. Nevertheless, we should discuss at least some general concepts related to digital recording. For a more complete description of the analog to digital conversion process, refer to chapter 4.

Digital audio recording uses numbers to represent the image of a waveform. With enough digits, the image will have such great resolution that it could be impossible to tell it from the original analog signal. A digital audio system typically involves analog to digital conversion, storage of digital data, digital

Scotch™

AVX/IRC Audio Cassettes

Technical Data

	Unit	C-10, C-20 C-30, C-46 C-60	C-90	C-120	Test Notes
PHYSICAL PROPERTIES					
Color: Oxide Side	—	Brown	Brown	Brown	—
Base Material	—	Tensilized Polyester	Tensilized Polyester	Tensilized Polyester	—
Standard Width	in (mm)	0.150 (3,81)	0.150 (3,81)	0.150 (3,81)	—
Width Tolerance	in (mm)	+0; −0.002 (+0; −0,05)	+0; −0.002 (+0; −0,05)	+0; −0.002 (+0; −0,05)	—
Nominal Thickness					1
Base	mil (μm)	0.45 (11,4)	0.29 (7,4)	0.23 (5,8)	—
Oxide Coating	mil (μm)	0.22 (5,6)	0.17 (4,3)	0.12 (3,1)	—
Total	mil (μm)	0.67 (17,0)	0.46 (11,7)	0.35 (8,9)	—
Static Tensile					2
Yield Strength	lbs/0.25 in (kg/6,3 mm)	1.9 (0,9)	1.2 (0,5)	0.8 (0,4)	2
Breaking Strength	lbs/0.25 in (kg/6,3 mm)	3.2 (1,4)	2.1 (1,0)	1.2 (0,5)	2
INTRINSIC MAGNETIC PROPERTIES					
Coercivity (Hc)	Oe (kA/m)	360 (28,7)	360 (28,7)	360 (28,7)	3
Retentivity (Br)	G (mT)	1400 (140,0)	1400 (140,0)	1600 (160,0)	3
Remanence (Ɽr)	Lines/0.25″ (nWb/m)	0.49 (780)	0.38 (600)	0.29 (460)	3
ELECTROMAGNETIC PROPERTIES					
Maximum Output Level					
315 Hz	dB	+5.0	+3.5	+0.5	4
10 kHz	dB	−8.0	−8.0	−8.0	5
Sensitivity					
315 Hz	dB	+0.5	−0.5	−3.5	6
10 kHz	dB	−1.0	−1.0	−3.0	6
Biased Noise Level, weighted	dB	−53.5	−53.5	−53.5	7
Signal-to-Noise Ratio	dB	59.0	57.0	54.0	8
Third Harmonic Distortion					
Level @ 250 nWb/m	% (dB)	0.6 (−45)	1.1 (−39)	2.5 (−32)	9
Test Conditions					
Tape Speed	ips (mm/s)	1⅞ (4,76)	1⅞ (4,76)	1⅞ (4,76)	—
Reference Fluxivity	nWb/m	250	250	250	—
Record Head Gap Length	mils (μm)	0.12 (3)	0.12 (3)	0.12 (3)	—
Reproduce Equalization	μsec	120,3180	120,3180	120,3180	—
Track Width	mils (mm)	24 (0,6)	24 (0,6)	24 (0,6)	—
Reference Tape	—	R723DG	R723DG	R723DG	—
Bias Level Relative to IEC Reference Tape	dB	0	0	0	—

Sensitivity vs. bias curves drawn using constant current recording (no record equalization).

GENERAL NOTE: The technical data for the products described are averages based on information accumulated during their life and are not to be used in the generation of purchase specifications which define property limits rather than typical performance. Data taken from a limited sampling may produce average figures differing from those quoted by as much as ±10% or ±1 dB (as applicable). Except where otherwise noted, tests are conducted at an ambient temperature of 70±5°F. and relative humidity of 50 ±5%. All statements, technical information and recommendations contained herein are based on tests we believe to be reliable, but the accuracy or completeness thereof is not guaranteed.

Figure 8.3 Typical technical specifications of tape. (Source: Magnetic Media Division/3M. St. Paul, MN. Reprinted with permission of and copyright by Minnesota Mining and Manufacturing Company.)

signal processing, and digital to analog conversion. The A/D conversion is done by sampling the analog signal many times a second (referred to as the sample rate) and generating a number to represent the analog waveform for each sample. The rate at which the analog waveform is sampled (32K, 44.1K, or 48K) determines the highest frequency that can be reproduced by converting the binary numbers back to an analog waveform. The highest frequency that can be reproduced is one half of the sample rate (i.e., for 32K, 44.1K, and 48K, the highest frequency that can be reproduced is 16K, 22.05K, and 24K, respectively. This determines the frequency response of the digital recording mechanism. The number of bits (see chapter 4) used to determine the value of each sample will determine the dynamic range (difference between softest and loudest sounds) and the signal to noise ratio (S/N). Using 16 bits for each sample (as normal mode DAT does) gives a range of values from 0 to 65,534 and results in S/N and dynamic range figures of 96 dB. Conventional analog tape recordings are able to support a dynamic range of only 65 dB.

The process of actually recording the digital information to the tape differs depending on the type of system. One solution is to use a rotary-head format, where the read/write head spins diagonally across the tape (helical scan). This is the way that VCRs are able to store their data to tape. Some decks are able to use stationary heads but tend to have wider tape and faster tape speeds. Most decks appear to be a cross between a typical analog cassette deck and a compact disc player. In addition to the primary signal, one can record subcode information such as the number of the track (so one can jump between recorded information in a certain order) or absolute time (counted from the beginning of the tape). The tape speed is much faster than a regular deck (one can rewind 30 minutes of recorded information in 10–25 seconds). Decks have analog inputs and outputs like on a regular tape player; they also have digital I/O. This allows one to make a copy onto another DAT deck directly (without having the music converted to analog and then reconverted to digital). This will make perfect copies because all that is transferred is numbers (no music or speech that can be distorted).

As the digital tape recorder is similar in technology to a video recorder, so too is the tape similar to a video tape. The tape shell is about half the size of an analog cassette and is protected by a hinged door like a videotape. Upon playing, the door is opened and the tape pulled out and wrapped around the spinning head. A tape can be as long as 90 or 120 minutes, and because there is only one "side" to the tape it is uninterrupted playing time. The actual recording time is determined by the sampling rate and the number of channels of information recorded.

PROPER RECORDING TECHNIQUE

Proper recording technique is not difficult to master. With a minimum of practice, you should be able to make acceptable recordings for any purpose.

You must decide what the purposes of your recordings are to be so that you can determine your best approach. Some of the questions you must answer follow.

Will the playback be for noncritical listening, or will a critical measurement approach be made? Recordings made for noncritical listening of events such as speech do not require the same high fidelity as those that are intended to be measured more closely. You could, for instance, economize on the tape you purchase for this kind of recording. Mouth-to-microphone distance need not be carefully controlled, and record level need not be monitored closely. If the intention is to critically evaluate some event, however, you would be wise to record on the highest quality tape to ensure the best possible signal-to-noise ratio. Use the highest recording speed allowed unless the playback and analysis will be done at a speed faster than the record speed. If this is to be the case, choose a record speed that will allow for an even higher playback speed. If this procedure is to be used, a careful analysis of the tape transport speed is a must to avoid introducing nonlinear frequency shifts to the data. Carefully monitor record level to prevent the possibility of print-through, but at the same time ensure that there will be sufficient recording strength to allow the signal to be passed through additional equipment in the analysis phase. You can usually do this by keeping the record level indicators (meter needle or lights) in the middle of their range. Never allow these indicators to range into the red or over-record area. Constant mouth-to-mike distance is a must if the recording is of speech and if critical measures are to be made at reproduction.

What is the nature of the signal to be recorded? Do I have some prior knowledge of the complexity of the spectrum and the amplitude? These questions bear directly on the quality of the tape and the speed of tape transport. Record signals (e.g., music) that have wide dynamic fluctuations in their intensities should be recorded at fast speeds to preserve their high frequency spectra. You should also record them on low-noise tape so that when the strength of the signal is at a minimum, background noise will not become a problem to the analysis routines.

What is the nature of the environment in which the recording will be made? In general, make audio tape recordings in quiet environments so that all that is recorded is the signal you wish to capture. If fine measures are to be made, you need to record the signals in an acoustically treated room. This is not a problem when the signal you need to record is an electrical event, such as a sinusoid from a function generator. In such a case, there is direct electrical connection between the two pieces of equipment, and no microphone is involved. If you need to record acoustic events in situations where the background noise cannot be reduced or controlled, consider the use of a directional microphone. This will at least ensure that there will be a favorable signal-to-noise ratio for the analysis phase.

SPLICING AND EDITING

Because tape is a serial storage/access medium rather than random storage/access (such as a floppy computer disk), you will frequently need to reorder material that is on the tape. This can be accomplished in at least two ways, editing and splicing.

First, you can use two recorders in such a way that those signals you want can be played back from one machine and rerecorded in the proper sequence on a new tape on the second machine. Editing is somewhat tedious and requires a good bit of concentration and physical coordination. For extensive reordering, it may not be the method of choice. **Splicing** is accomplished after cutting the tape into segments containing the relevant information and then joining it back together in the new sequence. This may seem simple, but it must be done correctly to prevent the segments from coming apart when you play them back. Figure 8.4 shows the basic splicing technique that you should use.

First, hold together the two pieces of tape that are to be joined, keeping the dark, or dull, sides facing in the same direction. Next, make a cut on about a 45-degree angle. Following that, bring the two ends of the tape together. Use splicing tape to create an inseparable joint. This may look easy, but it often is not. Figure 8.5 shows a splicing machine that virtually guarantees a good splice joint. The machine has clamps that can hold both of the free ends of the tape and a cutter that cuts on the required angle. Once you have made the cut, the clamps hold the cut ends in place until you can apply the splicing tape. Splicing

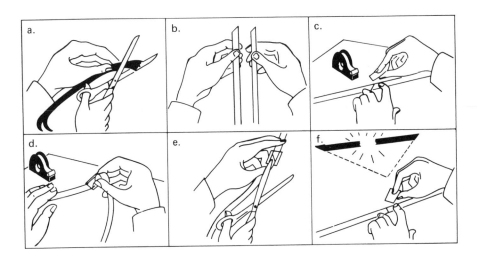

Figure 8.4 Splicing technique. (Source: *Elements of Magnetic Tape Recording* by N. M. Haynes, Englewood Cliffs, NJ: Prentice Hall, 1957, 1985. Reprinted with permission of the publisher.)

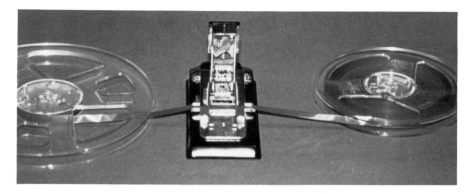

Figure 8.5   Splicing machine.

tape is usually a translucent white and uses a special adhesive. This adhesive, unlike that of regular pressure sensitive tape, will not flow and foul the tape heads with repeated use or unfavorable heat conditions. Always use splicing tape rather than common cellophane tape. Figure 8.6 shows several types of splice joints. Although each of the joints has advantages, the butt joint usually serves the largest variety of purposes and, with the aid of the splicing machine, is the easiest to perform.

TROUBLES AND REMEDIES

Occasional problems may arise with your recorder, and you may be able to fix some of these yourself. A quick check should reveal if a problem is something you can fix in-house or whether you will have to send the unit out for repair. Most problems involve incorrect connections or moving the wrong switch or control. The following list of problems and procedures is offered to help you locate some of the more common problems:

Recorder will not operate.

- Be sure that the power cord is in the wall and that there is power in the wall socket.
- Be sure that the recorder is switched on.
- Be sure that the tape is threaded across the playback heads properly. (Note: Some recorders are activated only when the tape is properly threaded across a tension bar that serves as an on/off switch.)
- Check fuse.

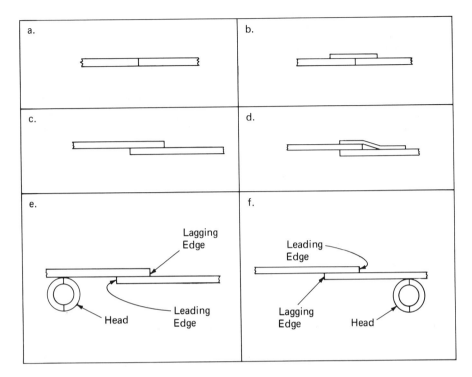

Figure 8.6 Types of splice joints: (a) butt-weld, (b) butt-strapped, (c) cement or weld-overlapped, (d) strapped-overlapped, (e) improper overlapped splice, (f) correct overlapped splice. (Source: *Elements of Magnetic Tape Recording* by N. M. Haynes. Englewood Cliffs, NJ: Prentice Hall, 1957, 1985. Reprinted with permission of the publisher.)

Recorder does not record.

- Be sure that the record switches are set to "record."
- Be sure that the signal to be recorded is reaching the recorder. Look for deflection on the volume unit meter.
- Be sure that the input wires are actually attached at the input of the recorder.
- Be sure that the record level controls have been turned up.
- Be sure that the source-tape switch is set to source.

Recorder does not play back.

- Be sure that the playback switches are on.
- Be sure that the source-tape switch is set to tape.

- Be sure that the output wires are actually connected to the output side of the recorder.
- Be sure that the playback levels have been turned up.
- Be sure that the tape is not blank.
- Check all patch cords.

Drop outs and distortion.

- Poor quality tape or tape that has been damaged.
- Poor quality recording.
- Dirty heads.
- Heads misaligned.
- Excessive record levels.
- Source information distorted before recording.
- Poor microphone.
- Worn heads.

MAINTENANCE

As the tape is transported across the heads, some of the magnetic material and the binder will be rubbed off onto the heads. Over time, these tend to accumulate and impair the recording quality. Head cleaner is available commercially, or you can use a small amount of denatured alcohol for this purpose. Simply wet a cotton swab in the cleaning solution and rub it carefully across the heads.

In addition to the deposits from the tape on the tape heads, the heads take on a magnetization characteristic of their own after repeated use. Once this has happened to the heads, they are capable of imparting that magnetic field to the tape even when the tape recorder is on playback. This problem is easily dispensed with by using a "head demagnetizer," a magnet that is powered by ordinary wall current. Bring the device into close proximity to the heads (do not touch them), and then slowly draw it away and turn it off. This process removes the residual magnetization. Beyond the cleaning and demagnetizing of the tape heads, there is little that you can do to the modern tape recorder to service it.

LABORATORY EXERCISE

In this exercise you will record a sustained vowel sound and then play it back into an oscilloscope for measurement of the fundamental period value. In addition, you will change the tape transport speed so that you may see that doubling the speed of the tape results in a doubling of the frequency of the signal. For this experiment you will need a microphone, a tape recorder, and an oscilloscope. Refer to Figure 8.7 for additional help.

Step 1.   Connect the microphone to the tape recorder using the "mic" input.

Step 2.   Begin the recording process, and adjust the record level until you are satisfied that you have a good record level. Proceed to record several seconds or even a minute of sustained vowel sound. (The vowel [a] would be a good choice.)

Step 3.   Connect the output of the tape recorder to the input of the oscilloscope; adjust the oscilloscope for free run.

Step 4.   Rewind the tape and start the playback into the oscilloscope. Adjust the vertical input sensitivity until you have a nearly full screen display.

Step 5.   Adjust the horizontal sensitivity on the scope until you can easily estimate the time between the major peaks in the vowel waveform.

Step 6.   Calculate the time between peaks and enter the time into the formula $f = 1/t$.

Step 7.   Rewind the tape again, and replay into scope at twice the tape speed. Recalculate the fundamental frequency of your voice, adjusting the

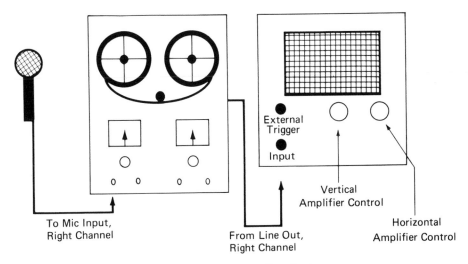

Figure 8.7 Equipment flowchart.

vertical and horizontal sensitivity of the scope if need be. If your tape recorder's transport is working properly, doubling the speed of playback should have doubled the frequency of the fundamental.

Note: If your laboratory has a frequency counter (a device for measuring and displaying the value of a pure tone), you can try this experiment again using a 1000 Hz pure tone to calculate just how accurate your tape transport speed really is.

KEY TERMS

carrier frequency	modulation
digital audio tape (DAT)	print-through
direct recording	splicing
drop-out	tape hiss
flutter	wow
frequency modulation	

SUGGESTED READINGS

Baken, R. J. *Clinical Measurement of Speech and Voice.* San Diego, CA: College-Hill Press, 1987.

Clifford, Martin. *Modern Audio Technology: A Handbook for Technicians and Engineers.* Englewood Cliffs, NJ: Prentice Hall, 1992.

McPherson, David L., and John W. Thatcher. *Instrumentation in the Hearing Sciences.* New York: Grune and Stratton, 1977.

Pohlmann, Ken C. *Principles of Digital Audio* (2nd ed.). Indianapolis, IN: Howard W. Sams, 1989.

Reed, Oliver. *The Recording and Reproduction of Sound.* Indianapolis: Howard W. Sams and Co, 1952.

CHAPTER 9

Sound Level Meters

In the audiology clinic, speech clinic, or laboratory, there is a continuing need to measure the intensity of sound. Sometimes this procedure is as simple as recording the level of the voice before beginning a recording. At other times the measurement may entail critical observations of the output of an audiometer or other device. In either case, a **sound level meter (SLM)** is an indispensable aid.

MEASUREMENT PROCESS

As you will remember from your courses in basic hearing science, sound amplitude can be expressed in at least two ways: **power or pressure.** The relationship between power, or intensity (I), and pressure (P) is shown in Equation 9.1.

$$I = P^2/Z_a \qquad \text{Eq. 9.1}$$

It is difficult to measure sound intensity directly because to do so means measuring the movement of the individual molecules of the medium (i.e., air). It is relatively easy to measure the sound amplitude, however, if one has an SLM because the meter has a pressure-sensitive microphone attached to it. The microphone converts the sound pressure at the diaphragm into electrical voltages. The voltage variations are then squared and divided by a value that is equal to the specific impedance of air (Z_a) Thus, the SLM has implemented

Equation 9.1, and the intensity of the sound can be read off the meter in dB sound pressure level (SPL) relative to 0.0002 dynes/cm^2. A **dyne** is the amount of force that will impart an acceleration of 1 cm per second per second to 1 g of mass.

Components and Controls

In its simplest form, the SLM is nothing more than a pressure-sensitive microphone attached to an electronic voltmeter. However, because measurements are usually made of both very weak and very intense signals, there must be additional circuitry that allows for altering the sensitivity range of the instrument. This is usually a wheel or knob that is marked off in steps of 10 dB and is used in conjunction with a display meter that can have a range of 20 or more decibels. For example, if the intensity setting is at 70 dB and the meter scale ranges from − 10 dB to 20 dB, this means that intensities from 60 dB to 90 dB can be measured without altering the sensitivity setting. Figure 9.1 shows a typical SLM.

In addition to the basic components discussed in the foregoing paragraph, there are usually options for other controls on the SLM. One such option is a means for controlling the meter needle display, such as a fast and a slow response speed. These settings alter the time constant of the SLM so that it follows most of the peaks in a variable amplitude signal (fast mode) or so that it averages across those peaks (slow mode). The choice of modes depends on some knowledge of the amplitude patterns of the signal being measured. Another option is **peak hold function** circuitry for measuring impulse signals. Many times the SLM will have provisions for implementing various sound weighting scales such as the A, B, or C scale of measurement. Discussion of the technicalities associated with the use of these scales is included later in this chapter.

Filter Sets

Although not always a part of the typical SLM, the octave band filter set is nevertheless a valuable addition. This set of one-octave filters attaches to the SLM and allows you to make measures of sound levels within a specified band of energy. This is particularly useful when using the SLM for calibration of pure tone signals and for work against a background of unwanted noise. Some meters have one-third-octave filters for use in more discrete noise analysis. Such a meter/filter combination can be used to analyze the sound levels made by a particular piece of factory equipment, for example.

CALIBRATION OF SOUND LEVEL METERS

If the SLM has not been calibrated, it will be of little use as a measurement device unless you want only relative information. Manufacturers of SLMs

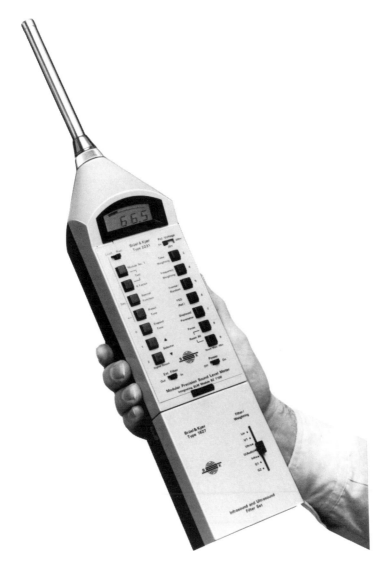

Figure 9.1   Sound level meter. (Source: Courtesy Bruel & Kjaer Instruments, Inc., Marlborough, MA)

provide a calibrated source of sound with their instruments. Two such sources are pictured in Figure 9.2. The **pistonphone** produces a broad-spectrum "buzzing" sound with peak energy at 250 Hz at about 124 dB. The sound level calibrator can produce several pure tones of differing levels. Whichever device you use, place it over the microphone of the SLM and turn it on. Then watch

Figure 9.2 Pistonphone and sound level calibrator. (Source: Courtesy Bruel & Kjaer Instruments, Inc., Marlborough, MA)

for the specified deflection on the meter. If the value is not correct, it is a simple matter to turn an adjusting screw until the appropriate SPL is recorded. Go through this simple procedure each time you use the SLM. Nothing is more frustrating than to have made detailed measures of sound levels only to find later that the values you have measured bear no relationship to the real phenomenon!

USE OF THE SOUND LEVEL METER

General Precautions

When you are using an SLM, always keep in mind that you are holding a very expensive piece of equipment. The cost of a reasonably good SLM is about $3,000; handle it with great care. The microphones too are expensive and can run from $800 to $1,000, or more. When you attach the microphones to the SLM or when you attach other parts, always take great care with the screw threads. These parts should turn with ease. If they do not, the last thing you want to do is to force one part onto another. This leads to "cross-threading" and expensive repair. When you use the SLM, it is also good practice to start with the instrument set to a rather insensitive position and to adjust to more sensitive positions as the sound level demands. This prevents high levels of sound from banging the meter's indicator needle against the extreme high end of its range. A final caution is that SLMs usually run on batteries; always turn an SLM off when it is not in use. Remember that the next person to come along does not want to find the meter dead.

Types of Measurements

Basically, the measurement uses of the SLM fall into two general categories: (1) making sound field measures, and (2) making pressure measures. Normally each of these applications requires the use of a different type of microphone. Various kinds of microphones are shown in Figure 9.3. The frequency response of the microphone is partially a function of the diameter of the diaphragm. Thus, for ultrasonic measurements, you might choose a $\frac{1}{8}$-in. microphone. Frequently $\frac{1}{2}$-in. microphones are used for sound field work and 1-inch microphones are used for pressure (earphone) measures. Technical and applications specifications are available from the manufacturers.

Sound Field Measurements.   Sound field measurements are those that are made of sound in an enclosure such as a room. Perhaps you need to know the intensity of the sound of a vacuum cleaner. This is an example of a sound field measurement and would require the use of the sound field or **field microphone**. After you have attached the microphone, calibrated the meter, and decided on the distance from the source at which the measurement is to be made, you can read the sound level of the vacuum cleaner off the face of the SLM. *Note:* The proximity of your body to the instrument will have noticeable effects on the final readout. Whenever possible, make sound field measures with the SLM attached to a tripod instead of holding it.

Should an octave band filter set be attached to your SLM, you can obtain further evaluation of the intensity by individual portions of the spectrum. Evaluation such as this would probably show that the vacuum cleaner was producing more low-frequency energy than high. To measure such a sound source, you can select the slow response setting so that you can get an overall average of the sound level. If you suspect variations in the vacuum's output

Figure 9.3 Various styles and sizes of condenser microphones. (Source: Courtesy Bruel & Kjaer Instruments, Inc., Marlborough, MA)

level, the fast setting would be more appropriate in revealing them. Another example of a field measurement is monitoring the voice level of a client who is in voice therapy. In such a case, it would be appropriate to use the meter on the fast setting so that the client could visualize the fluctuations in his or her vocal output.

Pressure Measurements. Pressure measurements usually entail the output levels of an earphone. The measurement is usually made over a mechanism that couples the earphone to the microphone of the SLM. For example, in the calibration of audiometric earphones, the phones are placed over a coupler with a volume of 6 cc, which is the approximate volume of air that is trapped between the diaphragm of the earphone and the tympanic membrane of the listener. In the case of the coupler (i.e., artificial ear), the earphone forms the outer limit of the 6 cc cavity and the SLM microphone serves as the tympanic membrane. Such a coupler arrangement is shown in Figure 9.4.

Another type of pressure measure that is frequently made is of the output of a hearing aid. This too calls for a **pressure microphone** to terminate a cavity volume. In this case the volume is 2 cc and approximates the volume of the human ear canal.

Probe Tube Measurements. Probe tube measurements are essentially pressure measures made inside a cavity that is usually too small to allow the use of a standard microphone (the ear canal or an oral cavity, for example), so a tube is attached to the microphone. The tube is introduced into the cavity, and

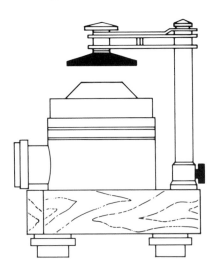

Figure 9.4 NBS 9A coupler (artificial ear). (Source: Courtesy Bruel & Kjaer Instruments, Inc., Marlborough, MA)

the microphone and SLM remain outside. (See Figure 3.9 for an example of a probe tube.) Because the addition of the tubing alters the frequency response of the microphone, recalibration is a must. Commercially available probe tube microphones have been calibrated to offset the effects of the tube.

WEIGHTING SCALES

As indicated previously, many SLMs have weighting scales to accommodate special types of measurement. Figure 9.5 (A, B, and C) shows the frequency sensitivity for each of these scales. It can be seen that if the A scale is turned upside down it looks very much like the response of the human ear to sound. This is intended because scales, or weighting factors, are used to simulate the human ear's response to low (A scale), medium (B scale), and high (C scale) sound levels. In your hearing or speech science courses you learned about the phon scale and phon contours. The A scale approximates the 40 phon contour, the B scale approximates the 70 phon contour, and the C scale approximates the 100 phon contour. If the sound level lies between 24 to 55 dB, use the A

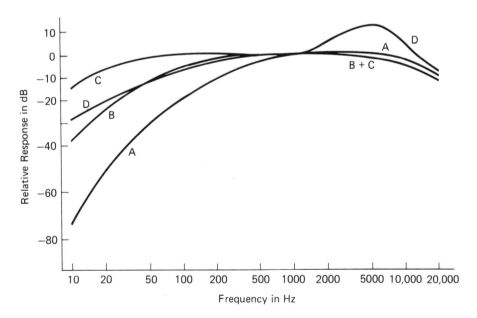

Figure 9.5 Frequency response of four weighting networks. (Source: *Instrumentation in the Hearing Sciences,* David L. McPherson. New York: Grune & Stratton, 1977, p. 152. Reprinted with permission.)

scale. If it is between 55 to 85 dB, use the B scale, and if it is over 85 dB, use the C scale to make noise level measures. If you find that the sound level on each of these scales is about the same, then most of the energy of the noise is at frequencies above about 500 Hz. If the sound level is the same on the B and C scale but is less on the A scale, then most of the energy is below 500 Hz. If the sound level is greatest on the C scale, the major area of energy lies below about 150 Hz. (Inspection of Figure 9.5 will reveal these relationships.) In practice, almost all sound level measures that are made with a weighting scale and are eventually related to human hearing are made on the A scale and reported as such (dBA).

USE OF THE SLM IN CALIBRATION OF AUDIOMETERS

A detailed discussion of audiometer calibration is not a topic for this text, but some mention of the use of the SLM in this activity must be made. Calibration of an audiometer involves more than just the calibration of the intensity of the output, and for those activities the SLM is not used. The SLM is indispensable for the calibration of intensity, harmonic distortion, attenuator linearity, and rise/fall time. For all these measures, the pressure microphone is used with the 6 cc cavity artificial ear. Calibration of the SLM should take place before beginning. Values for the parameters to be measured may be found in many textbook chapters on calibration or by directly consulting the American National Standards institute (ANSI) standard (ANSI S3.6, 1989). Table 9.1 shows a set of standard reference threshold sound pressure levels derived from this standard. Note that these pressure values are only valid for TDH-39 earphones. For values specific to other earphones the standard must be consulted.

TABLE 9.1
Standard Reference Threshold Sound Pressure Levels
From ANSI S3.6 – 1969

Frequency	Maximum Upper Limit of Hearing Threshold Level
125	45.5
250	25.5
500	11.5
1,000	7.0
1,500	6.5
2,000	9.0
3,000	10.0
4,000	9.5
6,000	15.5
8,000	13.0

Output Calibration

The measurement of output, **output calibration**, is fairly straightforward, involving only setting the attenuator of the audiometer at the appropriate setting (usually 70 dB hearing level [HL]) and then reading the dB values from the SLM. Make a note of plus or minus deviations from the standard for later reference. Values that are outside the allowable limits require that you recalibrate the audiometer.

Harmonic Distortion

Observation of **harmonic distortion** requires the use of an SLM and the octave band filter set. Set the phone over the coupler, and set the intensity to the level specified for that frequency by the standard. Then advance the filter setting one octave ahead of the signal coming from the audiometer. For instance, if the signal from the audiometer is 1,000 Hz, set the SLM filter to 2,000 Hz. When you do this, the fundamental (1,000 Hz) is rejected by the filter and the second harmonic (2,000 Hz) is passed. The difference between the level of the primary signal and the level of the harmonic can then be compared to the standard specification.

Attenuator Linearity

For **attenuator linearity**, you also set the phone over the coupler according to the specifications of ANSI. Reduce the attenuator settings by 10 dB steps and note the values each time on the SLM to determine if the reduction in SPL is linear. The standard specifies the limits of deviation from linearity.

Rise/Fall Time

You can measure the **rise/fall time** of the audiometer's signal without the aid of the SLM by simply routing the electrical output (before the earphone) to an oscilloscope. Then set the oscilloscope to trigger (see Chapter 7) at the onset of the signal when the interrupter is depressed. The primary flaw with this approach is that it does not reveal any deviations imposed on the rise time or the fall time by the earphone dynamics. To measure the acoustic rise and fall time, set the phone over the coupler and route the AC output of the SLM to the oscilloscope. The scope display then reveals the rise and fall time of the actual acoustic signal after transduction by the earphones. Measurement of the rise time and fall time requires a very brief time display on the face of the oscilloscope because these are events that are over within 25 to 100 msec. Manual triggering of this display with any degree of accuracy is impossible.

The simplest method of triggering is to split the output of the SLM, routing one patch cord to the input of the scope and the other to the scope trigger. You can also split off at the output of the audiometer so that the signal goes to the earphone and also to the scope trigger, which requires the use of either a mixer or a special splitting adapter. Either method ensures that the scope will be triggered at the instant the signal comes on. Of course, you will have to make some adjustment to the sensitivity of the trigger.

LABORATORY EXERCISE

In this exercise you will calibrate the SLM and then use it to measure the noise in a typical classroom. Besides an SLM, you will need a pistonphone to accomplish the calibration.

Step 1. Set up the SLM; it is usually a good idea to read the operations manual as you go along. The proper microphone for the type of measures to be made is the field microphone. If your lab does not have a field microphone, you may use a pressure microphone for purposes of this experiment. *Note:* Be very careful when attaching the microphone to the body of the SLM so that you do not strip the threads of either one.

Step 2. Place the pistonphone over the microphone, turn it on, and record the sound level on the SLM. If your SLM has an octave band filter attached to it, select the filter band width that corresponds to the frequency of the pistonphone output signal. If your SLM does not have the filter, use the linear setting or refer to the calibration instructions for the proper setting. Make any corrections that may be necessary to bring the SLM into calibration. Note: Usually the pistonphone's output frequency and amplitude (dB) will be noted somewhere on its surface. If not, consult the operations manual.

Step 3. Take the SLM into a classroom (either with or without people) and make measures of the sound levels. Make these measures on both the linear scale as well as the A scale so that you can see the difference. If there are differences between these two measures, what do those differences mean? (See the section on weighting scales in this chapter.)

Step 4. If your SLM has a series of one octave filters attached to it, you may also wish to make the measures over again at each of the filter settings. This will give you some idea of the spectrum of the noise in your classroom.

KEY TERMS

attenuator linearity	pistonphone
dyne	power

field microphone
harmonic distortion
output calibration
peak hold function
phon

pressure
pressure microphone
rise/fall time
sound level meter (SLM)

SUGGESTED READINGS

American National Standards Institute. *Standard Specifications for Audiometers*, ANSI S3.6–1989. New York: American National Standards Institute.

Bruel & Kjaer Co. *Instruction and Applications: Precision Sound Level Meters.* Cleveland, OH: Bruel & Kjaer Co., Reprinted 1964.

Melnick, William. "Instrumentation Calibration." In William Rintelmann (Ed.), *Hearing Assessment.* Baltimore: University Park Press, 1979.

Peterson, P. G., and E. E. Gross. *Handbook of Noise Measurement.* West Concord, MA: General Radio Company, 1967.

CHAPTER 10

Speech Physiology Instrumentation

In some of the previous chapters of this book we have already discussed instrumentation that can be used to study speech phenomena. Some specialized instruments have not been discussed, and they are important instruments for the beginning student to understand.

INSTRUMENTS FOR MEASURING RESPIRATORY FUNCTION

By analyzing the process of respiration during speech, you can record air pressure, airflow, volume of the lungs, movement of the chest and abdomen, and activities of muscles associated with respiration and articulation. Each of these phenomena could require that you use different instrumentation.

Air Pressure

One way to measure air pressure is to use a **manometer**. The dials of a manometer are usually calibrated to show pressure changes in terms of millimeters or centimeters of water. This unit of measurement is used because, historically, measurement of air pressure has been made relative to how far a column of water could be displaced. Figure 10.1 shows a manometer. Because the dials on this instrument must be read, it is best suited for static measures

Figure 10.1   Manometer.

of pressure, such as determining how much pressure a person can sustain by simply blowing into the manometer's mouthpiece. Such information could be useful for determining the overall strength of the pressure-building capability of someone with a neurological disorder such as cerebral palsy or someone with a defective velopharyngeal mechanism.

A somewhat simpler device for measuring air pressure is the U-tube manometer shown in Figure 10.2. In this instrument, an actual column of water is moved by the pressure generated, and the pressure is read off the calibrated markings on the backplate. This instrument is best suited to measurement of static pressure.

Figure 10.3 shows perhaps the simplest of all devices for measuring pressure. This device and its clinical use were described by Hixon (1982) and consists of a drinking straw, a paper clip, and a glass of water with 1 cm markings on the outside. It is assumed that an individual who can sustain pressure equal to 5 cm water for 5 sec has sufficient pressure for speech production. Accordingly, the straw is placed 5 cm beneath the water's surface, and the clinician asks the patient to sustain a stream of bubbles for 5 sec.

Pressure changes that occur during the act of speaking change very rapidly, and no measurement device with a dial or other markings exists that has enough speed to make the observations worthwhile for careful data collection. A different method of measurement must be used to measure pressure changes that occur within the oral cavity or within the nasal cavities during the ongoing process of speaking. For this kind of measure, the pressure changes must be

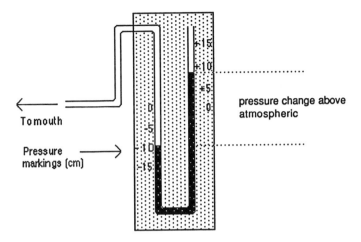

Figure 10.2   U-tube manometer showing increase over atmospheric pressure.

converted into electrical signals through the use of a pressure transducer, such as is shown in Figure 10.4.

Pressure transducers can be fitted to tubes that can be placed into the oral cavity, mounted in masks placed over the mouth and face, and even hung below the glottis to measure subglottic pressure. Another (although less pleasant) way to make subglottal pressure measurements is to attach the transducer to a hypodermic needle and then push the needle through the trachea just below the glottis. Because of the increased awareness of the rights of human subjects, this technique is rarely used.

The advantage of making measures of pressure with some sort of pressure transducer is that you can then store or display the pressure variations. For example, the electrical output of the transducer lends itself to being recorded on FM tape for later analysis. At some later time, the recording can be replayed and sent to an oscilloscope or a strip chart recorder for additional measurement. The pressure measurements can also be displayed in real time through the use of an oscilloscope for the benefit of a patient who is trying to modify pressure while in the act of speaking.

Air Flow

Whereas air pressure is a measure of force over area, air flow is a measure of volume per unit of time (i.e., milliliters per second). One air flow measurement device is called a **pneumotachograph**; it is pictured in Figure 10.5. This device is essentially a mask that fits over the face and has individual flow transducers

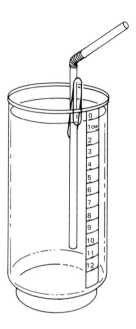

Figure 10.3 Simple manometer. (Source: "An Around-the-House Device for the Clinical Determination of Respiratory Driving Pressure: A Note on Making Simple Even Simpler," by Thomas J. Hixon, Jamet L. Hawley, and Kent J. Wilson. *Journal of Speech and Hearing Disorders, 47* (1982): 414. American Speech-Language-Hearing Association, Rockville, MD. Reprinted with permission.)

for both the volume of air leaving the oral cavity and that leaving the nasal cavity. The flow transducers are resistance devices and are therefore equally sensitive across the frequency spectrum. In addition, the transducers are differentially sensitive to pressure changes so that as long as the pressure on both sides of the transducer is the same no current will flow. The output of the pneumotachograph is then sent to a display device such as a strip chart recorder so that the changes in air flow can be displayed and measured. The instrument's output can also be directed to an FM tape recorder for later off-line analysis. Calibration of the pneumotachograph is accomplished by putting a known rate of air flow through it and adjusting the deflections on the strip chart or oscilloscope.

Lung Volume

Both the static and dynamic volume changes of the lungs can be measured through the use of a **spirometer**. A typical wet spirometer is pictured in Figure

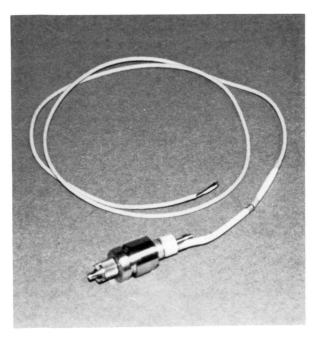

Figure 10.4   Typical pressure transducer.

10.6. Breathing into the mouthpiece of this instrument causes a plastic enclosure floating in water to rise and fall. The rise and fall of the enclosure is then translated into calibrated values of volume and marked on the associated strip chart record to chart measures of tidal volume and vital capacity.

To make volume measures during the act of speaking (which would be impossible with the spirometer), other instrumentation is available. For instance, you can use a **plethysmograph**, which is composed of a transducer that measures the changes in the cross-sectional area of the chest or abdomen that occur during breathing and speaking. The transducer is usually in the form of an elastic band that fits around the body; within the band is an inductor. As the chest wall or the abdomen expands and contracts, the changes in inductance are passed on to an amplifier and ultimately to a recorder, oscilloscope, or other display device. A typical plethysmograph called a Respitrace is pictured in Figure 10.7.

INSTRUMENTS FOR MEASURING LARYNGEAL FUNCTION

Over the history of the study of speech physiology and anatomy, several instruments have been designed for the observation of the vocal folds and

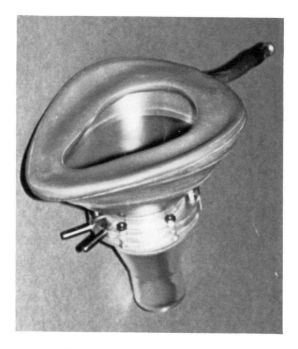

Figure 10.5 Pneumotachograph.

larynx. These devices have ranged from a simple mirror that could be held in the back of the throat so that light can be directed on the vocal folds **(laryngoscope)** to a fiberoptic system **(fiberscope)** that can be inserted into the nasal cavity and from which videotapes can be made of laryngeal activity. The laryngoscope is still used today in the modern practice of otolaryngology, but it has a major disadvantage in that the subject is not free to speak. Nevertheless, the laryngoscope used in conjunction with the high-speed camera has given us a great deal of our foundation data on laryngeal function.

The laryngoscope and the fiberscope are direct measures of function because the structures in question can actually be observed. There are, however, other more indirect methods for measuring laryngeal activity. One of these systems is called the **glottograph**, which works on the principle of **transillumination**. That is, a light source is placed on one side or the other (upper or lower) of the glottis, and a reflecting system is placed on the other side. The amount of reflected light then becomes a measure of the extent of the opening of the glottis. Obviously, a graph of the alternately greater or lesser amounts of light provides indirect information as to the periodicity of the opening and closing of the vocal folds.

Another instrument used for the indirect measure of the contact of the vocal

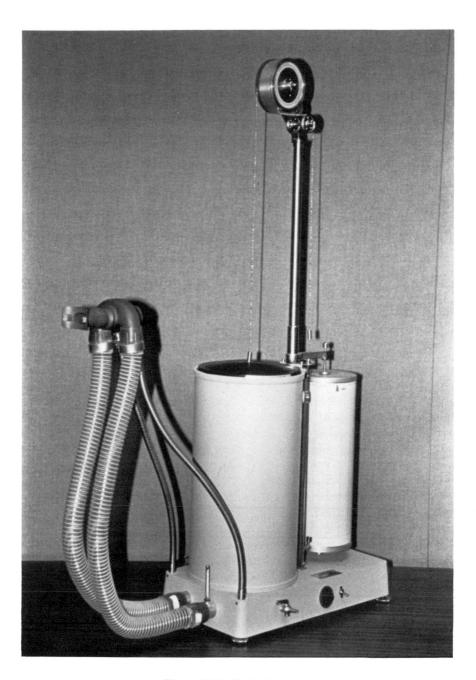

Figure 10.6 Wet spirometer.

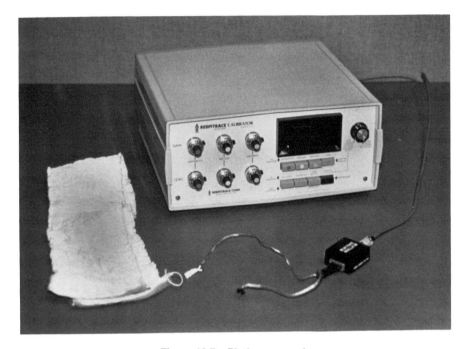

Figure 10.7   Plethysmograph.

folds is the **electroglottograph**, or Laryngograph, pictured in Figure 10.8. The electroglottograph works by measuring the change in conductance of a high-frequency signal passed across the throat by means of two small electrodes placed on either side of the larynx. When the glottis is closed, the current is conducted across the folds to the opposite electrode. When the glottis is open, the air space between the folds significantly increases the impedance between the electrodes, causing the signal to be reduced. This rise and fall of the signal represents the vocal fold contact and separation for each cycle and can be displayed in graphic form. Figure 10.9 illustrates the relationship between the transillumination of glottal width (photoglottogram) to the impedance change associated with vocal fold contact (electroglotto-gram). Examination shows that peak deflections on the electroglottogram curve correspond to maximum contact of the vocal folds on the photoglotto-gram curve. These points of maximum contact correspond to regions in which minimum amounts of light are detected by the photoglottogram transducer. From observation of these traces, it is a relatively simple matter to calculate the fundamental frequency of the voice with these techniques. All that is required is a calibrated time base for the graph. With that, the distance between the peaks can be calculated, converted to time, and the frequency of the Fo found (f = 1000/t). Other instrumentation such as the Visipitch system, PM Pitch

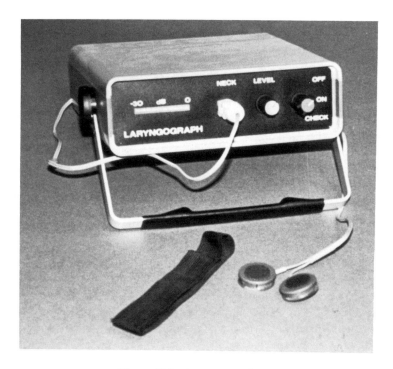

Figure 10.8   Laryngograph.

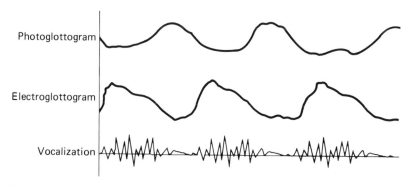

Figure 10.9   Comparison of data from photoglottogram and electroglottogram.

Analyzer system, and Micro Speech Lab system are commercially available for measuring the fundamental frequency of the voice. These systems and others like them are dedicated CRT display devices. In addition, several companies and individuals produce software for the purpose of measuring fundamental frequency and other aspects of the voice. This software is designed to be used with the more popular microcomputers.

INSTRUMENTS FOR MEASURING VELOPHARYNGEAL ACTIVITY

Nasal air flow as measured by, for example, a pneumotachograph can be used as an assessment of velopharyngeal activity, but air flow alone probably is not a reliable indicator of velopharyngeal patency. If you have obtained both air pressure and air flow measures, you can enter those values into formulas and use them to calculate such factors as velopharyngeal area and oral cavity constriction. Although convenient, formula approaches also have limitations.

Another useful approach in the clinical setting is the calculation of the ratio between oral and nasal sound pressures. Instrumentation is available that provides a measurement of oral/nasal sound pressure ratio during stop consonant production by microphonically measuring the sound at the nose and comparing it with that at the mouth. Because the velopharyngeal opening is normally closed during production of stop consonants, there is usually a relatively high oral/nasal sound pressure ratio. A low ratio suggests that the velopharyngeal port is open and signals the possibility of velopharyngeal incompetency. Other methods for indirect assessment of the velopharyngeal system have been proposed. There are suggestions for further reading on this subject at the end of this chapter.

The velopharyngeal system can be investigated more directly through the use of a fiberoptic system such as a Fiberscope. This system is based on the general instrumentation involved in endoscopy. It involves sending light through a bundle of fine glass fibers and observing the image that is then received through them. Because this bundle of glass fibers is flexible, the light can be directed into areas that would otherwise not be possible to see. With this technique, the vocal folds and the velopharyngeal opening can be viewed and videotaped through the instrument's eyepiece. The principal advantage to the fiberoptic approach is that it does away with the potential hazards involved with the use of X-ray to visualize these structures.

INSTRUMENTS FOR MEASURING MUSCLE ACTIVITY

The principal device to measure the muscle activity associated with the speech mechanism is called an **electromyograph (EMG).** All biological tissue, including muscle tissue, produces small electrical currents called **biopotentials**. The biopotentials can be picked up with electrodes; by amplification they can be recorded in a number of ways. The typical EMG recording is made by using very fine wires as electrodes. The wires are inserted into the muscles of the structures that are to be studied, and the electrical signals are led to the recording instrument. Fine wires are used because they do not hinder the use of the speech musculature, and recordings can be made without interfering with the speech process. The output of the EMG apparatus can then be sent to an FM recorder and/or to other display devices. In this way, you can study the interrelationship between the movements of the various muscle groups during the process of respiration, phonation, and articulation.

Electromyography can also be used as a method for training the speaker to gain better control of the speech musculature. When used in this way, it is usually referred to as **biofeedback**. The process of biofeedback consists of connecting electrodes coming from muscles to an amplifier and then providing some easy way for the subject to detect what the muscles are doing. One way is to cause the muscle biopotentials to raise and lower the pitch of a tone, which gives the subject instant feedback about how the muscles are operating.

Other methods for the study of the movements of structures associated with the production of speech (e.g., cinefluorography and tomography) involve the use of X-rays and are therefore potentially harmful. With the recent advent of ultrasonic imaging, the negative aspects of the X-ray can be overcome in displaying in real time the movements of structures involved in articulation. Ultrasonic imaging works very much like sonar in the sense that the echos from the primary signals provide the information necessary to reconstruct the view. Put more simply, a very high-frequency signal of short duration is emitted from the output transducer and travels through the portion of the body over which it has been placed. Reflections of the ultrasonic frequencies occur whenever the signal comes to a boundary between two structures. The reflections are reconstructed by computer assistance and displayed on a CRT.

With the use of the instrumentation discussed in this chapter, the modern clinician and speech scientist can make detailed and well-controlled observations of all aspects of the complicated process of speaking. In the clinical setting, it may be that only one or two of these instruments will be used at any given time. In the laboratory, however, several different instruments may be used simultaneously, each monitoring one aspect of the speech process.

LABORATORY EXERCISES

These exercises are designed to help you visualize some of the measurements and concepts discussed in this chapter. Because only instrumentation was discussed in this chapter and not the measurements made on the instruments, answers to the questions have been provided. These questions and answers are representative of the kinds of data that can be gathered using instrumentation of the type discussed in the chapter.

Exercise One

Figure 10.10 could be a typical CRT display or multiple trace oscilloscopic display of several events occurring simultaneously during the speech act. The

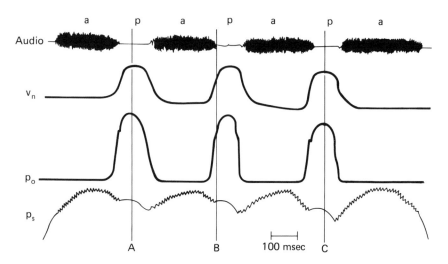

Figure 10.10 Display of events that occur during speech.

top trace (audio) is the audio record of the speaker producing [a pa pa pa]. The second trace (V_n) is the volume velocity of nasal airflow and represents the pressure difference developed as the nasal airflow passed through a pneumotachograph. The third trace (p_o) was obtained by placing an openended polyethelene tube in the mouth and connecting the tube to a pressure transducer. Finally, the subglottal pressure trace (p_s) was, in this case, collected by a pressure transducer connected to a hypodermic needle that had been inserted through the trachea below the level of the glottis.

Question 1. Where, during the production of speech, is the maximum intraoral pressure found?

Answer 1. Peak intra-oral pressure is found during the production of the [pa] at the time when the lips are closed. On the p_o tracing this is marked as point A.

Question 2. Where is the point at which the vibratory activity of the vocal folds stops?

Answer 2. Vocal fold activity stops at a point about two thirds of the way into the buildup of intra-oral air pressure, or at point B on the P_s tracing.

Question 3. Where is the point at which the nasal airflow is increased to a maximum?

Answer 3. Nasal airflow is at maximum at the point at which the production of the [p] causes the intro-oral air pressure to be at maximum. This is point C on the V_n tracing.

Exercise Two

This experiment is similar to Exercise One and illustrates the relationship between certain aspects of the speech act during the production of a vowel–unvoiced consonant–vowel ([apa]) and a vowel–voiced consonant––vowel ([aba]) contrast. For this exercise, look at Figure 10.11. Once again, P_s

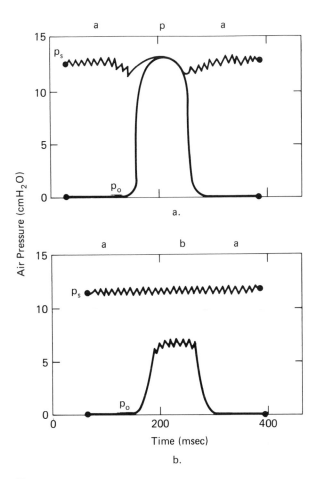

Figure 10.11 The relationship of (a) [apa] and (b) [aba].

represents the subglottal air pressure, and P_o represents the intra-oral air pressure.

Question. How would you describe the difference between the production of [apa] and [aba]?

Answer. Two aspects of difference are obvious. First, the rapid pressure variations in subglottic air pressure caused by the movement of the vocal folds does not cease during the production of [aba]. Second, intra-oral air pressure does not rise as high during the production of [aba] as it does during [apa], and the pressure variations caused by vocal fold vibration can be seen superimposed on the oral pressure tracing as voicing continues through the production of [aba].

KEY TERMS

biofeedback	laryngoscope
biopotential	manometer
electroglottograph	plethysmograph
electromyograph (EMG)	pneumotachograph
fiberscope	spirometer
glottograph	transillumination

SUGGESTED READINGS

Abbs, J. H., and K. L. Watkin. "Instrumentation for the Study of Speech Physiology." In N. J. Lass (Ed.), *Contemporary Issues in Experimental Phonetics.* New York: Academic Press, 1976.

Baken, R. J. *Clinical Measurement of Speech and Voice.* San Diego, CA: College-Hill Press, 1987.

Hixon, T. J., J. L. Hawley, and K. J. Wilson. "An Around the House Device for the Clinical Determination of Respiratory Driving Pressure: A Note on Making Simple Even Simpler." *Journal of Speech and Hearing Disorders, 47,* 413–415, 1982.

Lieberman, Philip. *Speech Physiology and Acoustic Phonetics: An Introduction.* New York: Macmillan, 1977.

Malmstadt, Howard V., Christie G. Enke, and Stanley R. Crouch. *Electronics and Instrumentation for Scientists,* Menlo Park, CA : Benjamin/Cummings Publishing Co., 1981.

Netsell, Ronald. *A Neurobiologic View of Speech Production and the Dysarthrias.* San Diego, CA: College-Hill Press, 1986.

Netsell, R., W. K. Lotz, and S. M. Barlow. "A Speech Pysiology Examination for Individuals With Dysarthria." In K. Yorkston and D. Beukelman (Eds.), *Recent Advances in Clinical Dysarthria.* Boston: College-Hill Press, 1989.

Pickett, J. M. *The Sounds of Speech Communication.* Baltimore: University Park Press, 1980.

Sithern, J., and T. Hixon. "A Clinical Method for Estimating Laryngeal Airway." *Journal of*

Speech and Hearing Research, 46, 138–146, 1981.

Warren, D. W. "Velopharyngeal Orifice Size and Upper Pharyngeal Pressure-Flow Patterns in Normal Speech." *Plastic and Reconstructive Surgery, 33,* 148–162, 1964.

Weismer, G. "Speech Breathing: Contemporary Views and Findings." In R. Daniloff (Ed.), *Speech Science: Recent Advances.* San Diego, CA: College-Hill Press, 1985.

Glossary

accelerometer: A device for measuring change in motion (acceleration). (Chapter 3)

active filter: Filter circuits containing amplifiers, resistors, and capacitors. (Chapter 6)

aliasing: "False" signals created when the A/D rate is less than twice the period of the highest frequency in the signal being digitized. (Chapter 4)

alternating current (AC): The most common form of electrical energy. Voltage and current are constantly changing in magnitude and periodically changing in the direction of flow. (Chapter 1)

ampere (amp): Metric unit for current. A unit of flow of current over time. (Chapter 1)

amplifier: A device for increasing the magnitude of a signal. (Chapter 6)

amplitude spectrum: A frequency domain plot showing the amplitude of individual frequency components. (Chapter 5)

analog event: A physical event that can consist of any value. Examples include temperature, pressure, and velocity. (Chapter 4)

analog filter: A filter that both inputs and outputs "real world" electrical events. (Chapter 6)

anode: In a CRT, the positive pole or attraction for the electrons released by the cathode. (Chapter 7)

attenuator: A resistance circuit designed to reduce the amplitude of a signal in predetermined and calibrated steps. (Chapter 9)

attenuator linearity: The quality of an attenuator that allows it to make equal reductions to signal strength for progressive attenuator settings. (Chapter 9)

band pass filter: A filter that passes signals that fall between two cutoff frequencies. (Chapter 6)

band reject filter: A filter that blocks signals that fall between two cutoff frequencies. (Chapter 6)

biofeedback: A process of using acoustic or visual feedback about the activity of muscles or other systems in the body. (Chapter 10)

biopotential: A voltage given off by the cells of the body and caused by ions. (Chapter 10)

bit: A bit is one of eight places in a digital word. A bit will have either Logic 0 or Logic 1. (Chapter 4)

capacitance: One of three components of impedance. A capacitor is an electrical device that offers increasingly less opposition to the flow of current as the frequency of that current increases. (Chapter 1)

capacitive reactance: Capacitive reactance acts to impede the flow of low-frequency current in a circuit. (Chapter 1)

carrier frequency: A signal (usually high frequency) against which other signals are modulated. (Chapter 8)

cathode: In a CRT, the source of the electrons for the light beam. (Chapter 7)

cathode follower: An amplifier circuit used in certain condenser microphones. (Chapter 3)

cathode ray tube (CRT): A vacuum tube producing a light beam display by means of an electron gun. (Chapter 7)

coaxial cable: Wire that has a central conductor with wire mesh wrapped around it. Useful for reducing the amount of unwanted electrical interference. (Chapter 2)

conductor: Any wire or metal that offers little resistance to the flow of electrons. (Chapter 1)

coulomb (C): The metric measure for charge; the charge present on 6.24×10^{18} electrons or protons. (Chapter 1)

current (Q): The number of free electrons that pass through a given point divided by the time that it takes them to pass. (Chapter 1)

damping constant: The specific time constant involved in the reaction of a system, such as a meter needle, to an event. A high damping constant produces a meter needle that does not react quickly to rapidly changing events. (Chapter 7)

diaphragm: Thin metal membrane over which acoustic pressure is distributed in microphones. (Chapter 3)

differential amplification: Process by which signals that are not common to each other are amplified. (Chapter 6)

digital audio tape (DAT): Recording process that uses analog to digital conversion of the recorded event. (Chapter 8)

digital event: An event that is composed of discrete values that are usually expressed as two voltage states. (Chapter 4)

digital filter: A filter that inputs "real world" electrical events and outputs digitized electrical events. (Chapter 6)

digitizer resolution: The accuracy with which the A/D converter represents the changing amplitude information of the analog signal. (Chapter 4)

direct current (DC): The form of electrical current that is found in batteries. So long as the battery remains charged, the current remains constant with no change in amplitude or polarity. (Chapter 1)

direct recording: Any recording on which the transduced signal is recorded as fluctuations in amplitude and frequency of an electrical signal. (Chapter 8)

displacement transducer: A specific type of transducer designed to change either linear or angular motion into an electrical waveform. (Chapter 3)

drop-out: Places on a tape where metallic particles are absent. This leads to silent periods on playback which are especially noticeable when recording continuous signals such as pure tones. (Chapter 8)

dynamic range: The range between the noise floor of the equipment and the level at which the equipment begins to distort the input. (Chapter 3)

dyne: The amount of force that will impart an acceleration of 1 cm per second per second to 1 g of mass. (Chapter 9)

electrical circuit: The wiring and other components through which electricity can travel. (Chapter 1)

electrical flux: The magnetic lines of force that surround a conductor in which current is flowing. (Chapter 1)

electroglottograph: A device for measuring the impedance change across the glottis. (Chapter 10)

electromyograph (EMG): A device for measuring electrical potentials produced by the muscles during movement. (Chapter 10)

electron: The negatively charged part of an atom. Some electrons are designated as "free" because they are bound loosely to the nucleus. (Chapter 1)

farad (F): The measure of the storage capacity of a capacitor. (Chapter 1)

Fast Fourier Transform (FFT): A process by which a complex waveform may be broken down and displayed as its individual frequency, amplitude, and phase components. (Chapter 5)

fiberscope: A device for observing the structures of the larynx and throat. Light is conducted through a series of fine, bendable glass rods. (Chapter 10)

field microphone: A type of microphone used in making measures in a sound field. The microphone automatically compensates for its presence in the field. (Chapter 9)

field of force: An electrical concept used to describe the energy field surrounding a positive charge. (Chapter 1)

filter: An electronic circuit or instrument that is designed either to reject or to pass certain frequencies or bands of frequencies in a signal's spectrum. (Chapter 6)

flutter: A type distortion involving tape transport speed changes of greater than 10 Hz. (Chapter 8)

flux: A solution used for cleaning metals that are to be joined by solder. (Chapter 2)

force: A concept involving mass times acceleration. (Chapter 1)

formant: Regions of energy prominence in the speech signal caused by vocal tract resonance. (Chapter 5)

free electrons: Electrons that are not tightly held to the nucleus and that are free to move to other atoms. (Chapter 1)

frequency domain: The spectral domain relating amplitude or phase to individual frequency components. (Chapter 5)

frequency modulation: A type of recording process for use in recording very low frequencies. (Chapter 8)

function generator: An instrument often used in the testing of other equipment. Capable of generating various types of waveforms of differing frequency. (Chapter 7)

gain: A value calculated by subtracting the input signal strength from the output signal strength. (Chapter 6)

glottograph: A device consisting of a subglottic light source and supraglottic light sensor that indirectly measures the opening and closing of the glottis by measuring the amount of light passing throughout the glottis. (Chapter 10)

ground: Connects the frame of the load device directly to the earth. Grounding can be accomplished by using three wire plugs on power line wire. (Chapter 1)

harmonic distortion: Distortion resulting when signals are present in the output waveform that were not present in the input waveform. (Chapter 9)

henry (H): The measure of the amount of inductance in an inductor. (Chapter 1)

hertz (Hz): A measure of the number of times per second that something alternates or repeats itself. In the United States, alternating current repeats at the rate of 60 Hz. (Chapter 1)

high pass filter: A filter that attenuates frequencies from DC to some cutoff and passes all others. (Chapter 6)

hysteresis: A measure of the ability of a device (transducer) to provide an exact representation of a continuum of change whether that change is from a low to high or high to low quantity. (Chapter 3)

impedance: The opposition to the flow of current in an electrical circuit. Impedance is composed of two parts: the resistive part and the reactive part. The reactive part changes with the frequency of the signal and the resistive part does not. (Chapter 2)

impedance matching: The process of making sure that there is compatibility between the input and output electrical characteristics of instruments. (Chapter 2)

in parallel: Meaning the electricity has more than one path to follow through the circuit. (Chapter 2)

in series: Meaning the electricity has only one path to follow through the circuit. (Chapter 2)

inductance: One of the components of impedance. An inductor is an electrical device that offers increasingly more opposition to the flow of current as the frequency of that current rises. (Chapter 1)

inductive reactance: Inductive reactance acts to impede the flow of high-frequency current in a circuit. (Chapter 1)

input: Information that the computer or other device receives from an external source. (Chapter 4)

insulator: A device with atoms so closely packed that there are no free electrons and thus no current flow through the material. (Chapter 1)

joule (J): A metric measure of work. The amount of work done by the force of one newton moving through a distance of 1 m. (Chapter 1)

laryngoscope: An angled mirror invented by Manuel Patrico Rodriguez Garcia in 1854 for the direct visualization of the vocal folds. (Chapter 10)

load: A device that uses electrical energy and converts it to some other form (e.g., light or heat). (Chapter 1)

Logic 0: One of two binary (digital) states, usually consisting of 0.0 to 0.8 v. (Chapter 4)

Logic 1: One of two binary (digital) states, usually consisting of 2.5 to 5.0 v. (Chapter 4)

low pass filter: A filter that passes frequencies from its cutoff down to DC. (Chapter 6)

manometer: A device for the measurement of static air pressure. (Chapter 10)

mixer: An electrical circuit or instrument that is designed to allow two or more signals to be mixed together without any accompanying impedance mismatch problems. (Chapter 6)

modulation: A type of recording distortion resulting in a fuzzy sound. May be caused by overrecording the input signal. (Chapter 8)

multiplexing: A process of time sharing by which the computer is able to rapidly sample many input lines on a rotating basis. (Chapter 4)

neutron: An atomic particle with a neutral charge or no charge. (Chapter 1)

newton: A measure of force. 1N = 0.225 lb. (Chapter 1)

noise floor: The level below which meaningful measures of a phenomenon can no longer be made because they are less intense than the internal noise of the measuring device. (Chapter 3)

ohm (Ω): The measure of electrical resistance. Ohms equal voltage divided by current. (Chapter 1)

operational amplifier: An amplifier employing negative feedback techniques to control its amplifying effects. (Chapter 6)

oscilloscope: A CRT display device for showing amplitude against time plots of signals. (Chapter 7)

output: Information sent by the computer to an external source. (Chapter 4)

output calibration: The act of controlling or standardizing the output signal of some device. (Chapter 9)

parallel input/output: Data that comes into or goes out of the computer by groups of bits. (Chapter 4)

passive filter: A filter composed of a network of discrete resistance, capacitance, and inductance. (Chapter 6)

peak hold function: An option on some sound level meters that allows the direct reading of sound pressure level (SPL) for very short and impulsive stimuli. (Chapter 9)

phase spectrum: A frequency domain plot showing the phase of individual frequency components. (Chapter 5)

phon: A standard measure of loudness level. For example, 40 phons is the loudness of a 1,000 Hz tone at 40 dB SPL. (Chapter 9)

piezoelectric effect: A phenomenon caused by the bending or compressing of crystalline substances. When the faces of two crystals are fixed together, distortion will cause a small electrical current to flow. (Chapter 3)

pistonphone: A calibration device for use with sound level meters that outputs a known frequency and intensity. (Chapter 9)

plethysmograph: A device sensitive to changes in electrical inductance that may be fitted around the chest or abdomen and used to record changes associated with breathing and speaking. (Chapter 10)

pneumotachograph: A device with a differentially sensitive flow transducer fitted into a face mask that can be used to record the dynamic air flow changes that occur during speaking. (Chapter 10)

polarization voltage: A constant voltage applied to capacitive type microphones. (Chapter 3)

port: An input or output on a computer. May be serial or parallel. (Chapter 4)

potential energy: The work that a body or charge can do when moving from one point to another. (Chapter 1)

power: A concept that unifies the factors of force, distance, and time. Power refers to work done in some unit of time. The basic unit of power is the watt. (Chapter 1)

power amplifier: An instrument that is designed to boost the current in a signal so as to be able to operate a load consuming large amounts of power (e.g., loudspeakers). (Chapter 6)

preamplifier: An instrument designed for an initial increase in the voltage of a signal before passing that signal on to a power amplifier or other device. May also have provisions for conditioning the signal (e.g., tone control). (Chapter 6)

pressure: A concept that involves force working over a certain area. Pressure can be expressed in terms of dynes per centimeter. (Chapter 9)

pressure microphone: Microphone that is used to make measures of pressure. May be used in a coupler to make measures of the sound pressure level of earphones. (Chapters 3 and 9)

print-through: A process that usually occurs because the record level was set on high. Can also occur with the use of very thin tape. The signal that is recorded at one spot on the tape is imprinted on a neighboring layer of tape on the reel. The results are "ghost" signals either before or after the primary signal. (Chapter 8)

proton: A positively charged atomic particle. (Chapter 1)

real time analysis: Analysis of a signal that is done instantaneously as it is being received by the analyzing device. (Chapter 5)

resistance (r): A characteristic of some materials that lessens the flow of current through them. (Chapter 1)

resistive transducer: A specific type of transducer designed so that the material of its construction changes its resistance to the flow of electrical current as there are changes in the measured phenomenon (e.g., heat). (Chapter 3)

rise/fall time: The time required for a signal to rise and fall between 10% and 90% of its maxima and minima. (Chapter 9)

roll-off rate: The rate at which the signal intensity is reduced on either side of the cutoff frequency of a filter's pass band. (Chapter 6)

sampling rate: The rate at which an A/D device takes repeated samples of the incoming waveform. (Chapter 4)

semiconductor: A device with impurities in its material that allow for the controlled movement of electrons through the material. (Chapter 1)

serial input/output: Data that come into or goes out of the computer in a sequential fashion one bit at a time. (Chapter 4)

signal averaging: A technique of repeatedly sampling the same analog event in order to make that event stand out from a background of unwanted events. (Chapter 4)

solder: A metal composed of a mixture of tin and lead that is used to join two pieces of metal together. (Chapter 2)

sound level meter (SLM): A device for measuring the amplitude of sound. (Chapter 9)

source: The origin of the information or the input device. (Chapter 1)

spectrograph: A device for recording the frequency and time parameters of a signal. Usually used for analyzing speech waveforms. (Chapter 5)

spectrum: The relationship between amplitude, frequency, and phase at a particular point in time. (Chapter 5)

spectrum analysis: An analysis technique for visualizing the relative frequency and phase content of a signal. (Chapter 5)

spirometer: A device that can be used to record measures of lung volume and respiration. (Chapter 10)

splicing: A technique for joining cut ends of tape. Can be used to rearrange sections of tape. (Chapter 8)

step attenuator: An attenuator with discrete positions of attenuation; not continuous. (Chapter 6)

strain gauge: A specific type of displacement transducer. Can be applied for use wherever a bending type change (torsion) is to be measured. (Chapter 3)

strip chart recorder: A device for recording long-term signal events on a moving strip of paper by using a pen that moves on the Y-axis; the moving paper creates the X-axis. (Chapter 7)

switch: A device for turning on or off the flow of electricity in a circuit. (Chapter 1)

tape hiss: The random high-frequency noise that is produced by metal particles on the tape and heard during playback. (Chapter 8)

thermistor: A specific type of resistive transducer. Can be applied for use wherever temperature changes are to be measured. (Chapter 3)

time constant: The time required for an electrical circuit to react to a change in the input signal. (Chapter 6)

time domain: The spectral domain that relates the changing amplitude of the signal over time. (Chapter 5)

transducer: Any device that can faithfully alter the original form of energy change to an electrical representation of that change. (Chapter 3)

transduction: The process of changing or transducing one signal type into another (e.g., acoustic to electrical). (Chapter 3)

transfer function: The operating characteristic that relates the input of a system to its output. (Chapter 6)

transillumination: A technique used in conjunction with the glottograph to cause light to shine either from above or below the glottis. (Chapter 10)

transistor-transistor-logic (TTL): The type of logic voltages used by many computers. (Chapter 4)

triggering: A process of starting the capture of a signal at some specified moment in time. (Chapter 4)

voltage divider: An electrical circuit that reduces the amplitude of a signal by some known ratio. Voltage dividers serve as the building blocks for attenuators. (Chapter 6)

volts (voltage) (v): The "pressure" that causes current to flow between a point of high negativity to low negativity (positivity). (Chapter 1)

watts (wattage) (w): The unit measure of power consumed by the load. Wattage is calculated by multiplying the voltage by the amperage. Normally expressed in kilowatts or kilowatt hours (kwh). (Chapter 1)

weber (Wb): The measure of the strength of the electrical flux produced by a current. (Chapter 1)

Wheatstone bridge: A resistance circuit balanced in such a manner that an unknown resistance quantity introduced into the circuit can be quantified. (Chapter 3)

work: Done when a force acts through a distance. Work (ergs) = Force (dynes) × Distance (cm). (Chapter 1)

wow: A type of distortion involving tape transport speed changes of less than 10 Hz. (Chapter 8)

X–Y plotter: An output device for recording short-term signal events on a stationary piece of paper by using a pen that moves along both the X- and Y-axes. (Chapter 7)

Suggested Readings

Abbs, J. H., and K. L. Watkin. "Instrumentation for the Study of Speech Physiology." In N. J. Lass (Ed.), *Contemporary Issues in Experimental Phonetics*. New York: Academic Press, 1976.

American National Standards Institute. Standard Specifications for Audiometers, ANSI S3.6-1969 (R 1973). New York: American National Standards Institute, 1969.

Baken, R. J. *Clinical Measurement of Speech and Voice*. San Diego, CA: College-Hill Press, 1987.

Borden, Gloria J. *Speech Science Primer*. Baltimore: Williams & Wilkins, 1980.

Bruel & Kjaer Application Notes. "Measurements of Harmonics, Difference Frequencies, and Intermodulation Distortion." Cleveland, OH: Bruel & Kjaer Co.

Bruel & Kjaer Co. "Instruction and Applications: Precision Sound Level Meters." Cleveland, OH: Bruel & Kjaer Co., Reprinted 1964.

Bruel & Kjaer Co. "Microphones Used as Sound Sources," Technical Review, No. 3. Cleveland, OH: Bruel & Kjaer Co., 1977.

Carr, Joseph J. *The Complete Handbook of Amplifiers, Oscillators, and Multivibrators* (1st ed). Blue Ridge Summit, PA: Tab Books, 1981.

Clifford, Martin. *Modern Audio Technology : A Handbook for Technicians and Engineers,* Englewood Cliffs, NJ: Prentice Hall, 1992.

Coffron, James W. *The Apple Connection*. Berkeley, CA: Sybex, 1982.

Curtis, Jack F. *An Introduction to Microcomputers in Speech, Language, and Hearing*. Boston: Little, Brown, 1987.

Curtis, Jack F., and Martin C. Schultz. *Basic Laboratory Instrumentation for Speech and Hearing*. Boston: Little, Brown, 1986.

Davis, R. 0. "Digital Signal Processing in Studies of Animal Acoustical Communication Including Human Speech." *Computer Methods and Programs in Biomedicine, 23,* 171–196, 1986.

Davis, R. 0. "The Personal Acoustics Lab (PAL): A Microcomputer Based System for Digital Signal Acquisition, Analysis, and Synthesis." *Computer Methods and Programs in Biomedicine, 23,* 199–210, 1986.

Dawson, William L. *Instrumentation in the Speech Clinic*. Danville, IL: Interstate Printers & Publishers, 1973.

Decker, T.N. *Analog to Digital Conversion: It's Not a Religious Experience.* The Hearing Journal, May 1992.

Departments of the Army and Air Force. *Electrical Fundamentals.* Department of the Army Technical Manual (TM11-681) and Department of the Air Force Technical Order (TO 16-1-218). Departments of the Army and Air Force, 1976.

Grossfeld, M. L., and C. A. Grossfeld. *Microcomputer Applications in Rehabilitation of Communication Disorders.* Rockville, MD: Aspen Publishers, 1986.

Hicks, M. Robert, Jerald R. Schenken, and Mary Ann Steinrauf. *Laboratory Instrumentation,* edited by C.A. McWhorter. Hagerstown, MD: Harper & Row, 1980.

Hixon, T. J., J. L. Hawley, and K. J. Wilson. "An Around the House Device for the Clinical Determination of Respiratory Driving Pressure: A Note on Making Simple Even Simpler." *Journal of Speech and Hearing Disorders, 47,* 413–415, 1982.

Khazan, Alexander D. *Transducers and Their Elements: Design and Application.* Englewood Cliffs, NJ: Prentice Hall, 1994.

Lenk, John D. *Handbook of Oscilloscopes: Theory and Application.* Englewood Cliffs, NJ: Prentice-Hall, 1982.

Lieberman, Philip. *Speech Physiology and Acoustic Phonetics: An Introduction.* New York: Macmillan, 1977.

Malvino, Albert P. *Resistive and Reactive Circuits.* New York: McGraw-Hill, 1974.

McPherson, David L., and John W. Thatcher. *Instrumentation in the Hearing Sciences.* New York: Grune & Stratton, 1977.

Melnick, William. "Instrumentation Calibration." In William Rintelmann (Ed.), *Hearing Assessment.* Baltimore: University Park Press, 1979.

Netsell, Ronald. *A Neurobiologic View of Speech Production and the Dysarthrias.* San Diego, CA: College-Hill Press, 1986.

Netsell, R., W. K. Lotz, and S. M. Barlow. "A Speech Physiology Examination for Individuals With Dysarthria." In K. Yorkston and D. Beukelman (Eds.), *Recent Advances in Clinical Dysarthria.* Boston: College-Hill, 1989.

Peterson, P. G., and E. E. Gross. *Handbook of Noise Measurement.* West Concord, MA: General Radio Company, 1967.

Pickett, J. M. *The Sounds of Speech Communication.* Baltimore: University Park Press, 1980.

Pohlmann, Ken C. *Principles of Digital Audio (2nd ed).* Indianapolis, IN: Howard W. Sams, 1989.

Potter, R. K., G. Kopp, and H. Green. *Visible Speech.* New York: Van Nostrand Reinhold, 1947.

Reed, Oliver. *The Recording and Reproduction of Sound.* Indianapolis: Howard W. Sams and Co, 1952.

Rockland Systems Corp. "The Application of Filters to Analog and Digital Signal Processing," West Nyack, NY: Rockland Systems Corp., 1976.

Silverman, Franklin H. *Microcomputers in Speech-Language Pathology and Audiology: A Primer.* Englewood Cliffs, NJ: Prentice-Hall, 1987.

Sithern, J., and T. Hixon. "A Clinical Method for Estimating Laryngeal Airway." *Journal of Speech and Hearing Research, 46,* 138–146, 1981.

Stearns, Samuel D., and Don R. Hush *Digital Signal Analysis (2nd ed).* Englewood Cliffs, NJ: Prentice-Hall, 1990.

Strong, Peter. *Biophysical Measurement.* Beaverton, OR: Tektronix, Inc., 1970.

Varoba, Barry. *Experiments in the Hearing and Speech Sciences.* Eden Prairie, MN: Starkey Laboratories, 1978.

Warren, D. W. "Velopharyngeal Orifice Size and Upper Pharyngeal Pressure-Flow Patterns in Normal Speech." *Plastic and Reconstructive Surgery, 33,* 148–162, 1964.

Weismer, G. "Speech Breathing: Contemporary Views and Findings." In R. Daniloff (Ed.), *Speech Science: Recent Advances.* San Diego, CA: College-Hill Press, 1985.

Young, Stephen. *Electronics in the Life Sciences.* New York: Halsted Press, 1973.

Index